THE WEAPONS ENCYCLOPÆDIA
TANK AIRCRAFT AFV SHIP ARTILLERY VEHICLES SECRET WEAPON
SPECIAL ALBUM

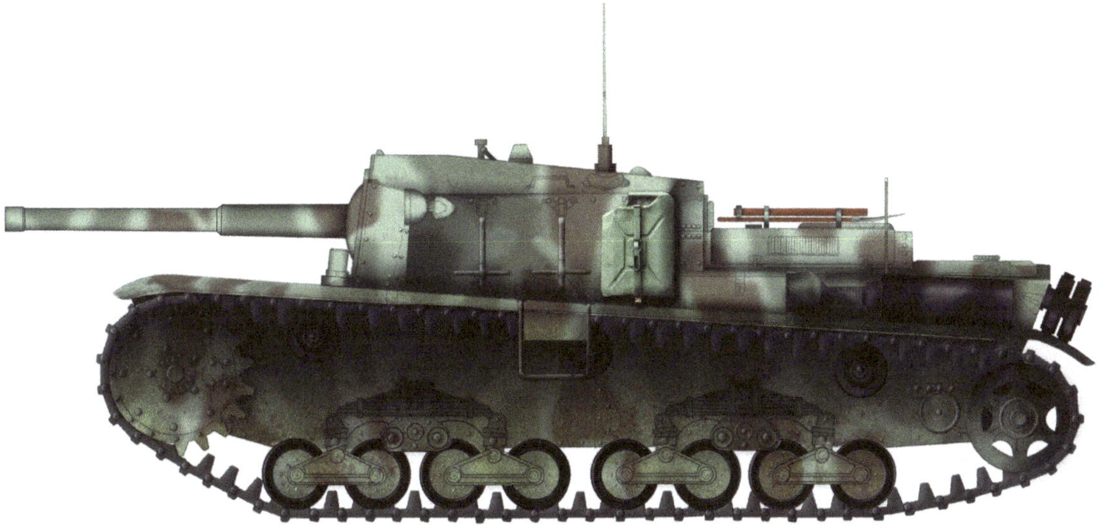

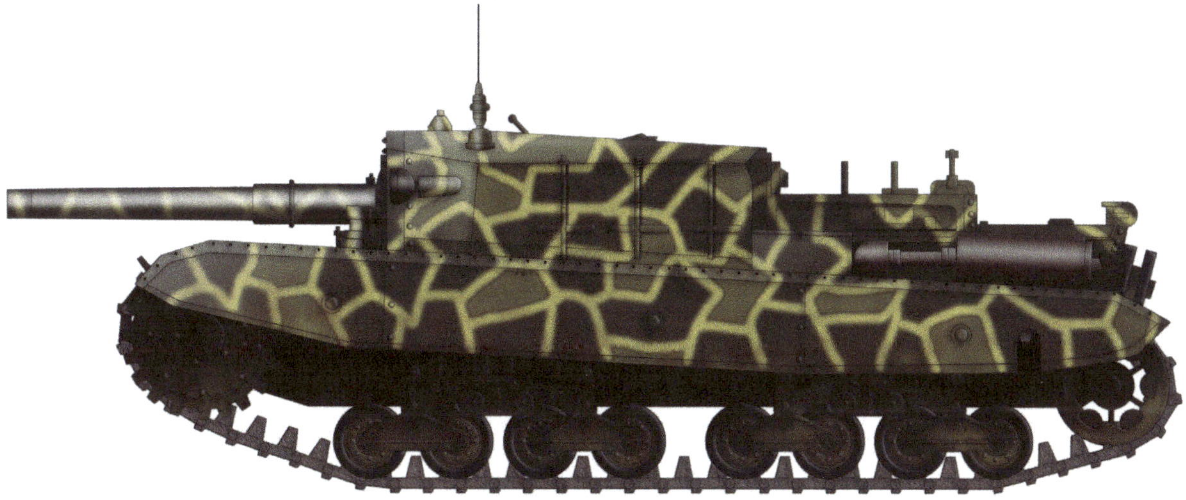

TWE-A1 ENG

ITALIAN SEMOVENTI WWII

THE WEAPONS ENCYCLOPAEDIA

EDITORIAL STAFF
Luca Cristini, Paolo Crippa.

ACADEMIC STAFF
Enrico Acerbi, Massimiliano Afiero, Aldo Antonicelli, Ruggero Calò, Luigi Carretta, Flavio Chistè, Anna Cristini, Carlo Cucut, Salvo Fagone, Enrico Finazzer, Arturo Giusti, Björn Huber, Andrea Lombardi, Aymeric Lopez, Marco Lucchetti, Gabriele Malavoglia, Luigi Manes, Giovanni Maressi, Francesco Mattesini, Daniele Notaro, Péter Mujzer, Federico Peirani, Alberto Peruffo, Maurizio Raggi, Andrea Alberto Tallillo, Antonio Tallillo, Roberto Vela, Massimo Zorza.

PUBLISHED BY
Luca Cristini Editore (Soldiershop), via Orio, 35/4 - 24050 Zanica (BG) ITALY.

DISTRIBUTION BY
Soldiershop - www.soldiershop.com, Amazon, Ingram Spark, Berliner Zinnfigurem (D), LaFeltrinelli, Mondadori, Libera Editorial (Spain), Google book (eBook), Kobo, (eBoook), Apple Book (eBook).

PUBLISHING'S NOTES
None of unpublished images or text of our book may be reproduced in any format without the expressed written permission of Luca Cristini Editore (already Soldiershop.com) when not indicate as marked with license creative commons 3.0 or 4.0. Luca Cristini Editore has made every reasonable effort to locate, contact and acknowledge rights holders and to correctly apply terms and conditions to Content. Every effort has been made to trace the copyright of all the photographs. If there are unintentional omissions, please contact the publisher in writing at: info@soldiershop.com, who will correct all subsequent editions.

LICENSES COMMONS
This book may utilize part of material marked with license creative commons 3.0 or 4.0 (CC BY 4.0), (CC BY-ND 4.0), (CC BY-SA 4.0) or (CC0 1.0). We give appropriate attribution credit and indicate if change were made in the acknowledgments field. Our WTW books series utilize only fonts licensed under the SIL Open Font License or other free use license.

CONTRIBUTORS OF THIS VOLUME & ACKNOWLEDGEMENTS
We would like to thank the main contributors to this issue: Arturo Giusti, whose articles made life less difficult in preparing the texts of the first chapters on the self-propelled L3 and L640. The wagon profiles are all by the author. The colouring of the photos is by Anna Cristini. Special thanks to national and/or private institutions such as: Army General Staff, State Archives, Bundesarchiv, Nara, Library of Congress, Wikipedia, USAF, Signal magazine, War Chronicles, War Front, IWM, Australian War Museum, etc. A P.Crippa, A.Lopez, L.Manes, C.Cucut, Tallillo archives. Model Victoria (www.modelvictoria.it) etc. for providing images or other items from their archives.

For a complete list of Soldiershop titles, or for every information please contact us on our website: www.soldiershop.com or www.cristinieditore.com. E-mail: info@soldiershop.com. Keep up to date on Facebook https://www.facebook.com/soldiershop.publishing

Title: **ITALIAN SEMOVENTI WWII** Code.: **TWE-A1 EN** Series by L. S. Cristini
ISBN code: 9791255892007. First edition January 2025
THE WEAPONS ENCYCLOPAEDIA (SOLDIERSHOP) is a trademark of Luca Cristini Editore

THE WEAPONS ENCYCLOPÆDIA
TANK AIRCRAFT AFV SHIP ARTILLERY VEHICLES SECRET WEAPON SPECIAL ALBUM

ITALIAN SEMOVENTI WWII

LUCA STEFANO CRISTINI

BOOK SERIES FOR MODELERS & COLLECTORS

CONTENTS

Preface 5
The Italian semoventi 5
The first prototypes 7
From Renault FT to Semovente L3 7
Semovente Moto Guzzi 9
Technical features 10
Ansaldo 9 Ton Self-Propelled 13
Technical features 13
Semovente L3 47/32 19
Technical features 20
Semovente B1 Bis (France) 26
Semovente L40 47/32 27
Technical features 32
Semovente 75/18 35
Technical features 40
Versions of the vehicle 45
Operational use 51
Production and export 63
The "anti-aircraft" semovente 73

Semovente 75/34 75
Technical features 77
Semovente 75/46 83
Technical features 83
Semovente 102/25 91
Technical features 92
Semovente 90/53 99
Technical features 100
Semovente 149/40 107
Technical features 100
Operational use 111
Modellism and self-propelled 114
Camouflage and markings 115
Bibliography 116

▲ Semovente 75/18 M.41 on display in Via dei Fori Imperiali in Rome. CC1

PREFACE

THE ITALIAN SEMOVENTI

It was especially during the Second World War that interest in self-propelled guns, armoured vehicles without turrets but equipped with powerful casemate-mounted cannons, spread to several countries, *primarily* following the example of Germany.

Italy also undertook the development of these vehicles, at first mainly derived from the M13/40 tank. The first models, equipped with 75/18 mm cannons, quickly proved their effectiveness, as was well demonstrated by the numerous tests, also carried out in the Libyan desert by Captain Traniello. All tests extolled their usefulness both as support artillery and as an anti-tank weapon, emphasising their power and ease of concealment, which made them appreciated and considered even by their adversaries.

These self-propelled vehicles, although designed and produced to support the operations of the Royal Italian Army, continued to be used even after the armistice of 8 September 1943, when several captured examples were successfully integrated into the Wehrmacht.

Their simple design and versatility made them suitable for various functions, but the delay in development and production greatly limited their strategic impact.

Alongside models based on the M13/40 hull, other self-propelled vehicles were developed from the M15/42 tank, with the introduction of more powerful guns, such as the 75/34 and later the 75/46, the latter mounted on vehicles with increasingly thicker and more advanced armour. Among the most powerful was the 105/25 M43, a self-propelled gun capable of competing with the most modern tanks of the time. However, the very limited production and the delay in its operational deployment reduced its overall effectiveness in the conflict.

An emblematic case of the challenges faced by Italian war production is the 90/53 self-propelled gun, designed on the modified hull of the M15 tank. Equipped with a 90 mm anti-aircraft gun, this vehicle was comparable to the famous German 88, excelling in initial projectile speed. Despite its potential, mechanical and logistical problems, coupled with a shortage of resources, limited its use. Of the thirty units produced, only a few reached the front, mainly in Sicily, where they demonstrated high accuracy and firepower but also ended up suffering heavy losses.

The parable of Italian self-propelled vehicles reflected and highlighted the strengths and weaknesses of the national war industry: extraordinary guns, but undersized engines and unreliable mechanics. Produced in limited numbers and often too late to influence the outcome of the conflict, these vehicles nevertheless represent a significant contribution to the history of Italian military technology.

▲ Two 47/32 L40 self-propelled tanks in action in the Libyan desert (author's colouring).

ITALIAN SEMOVENTI 1919-1945

THE FIRST PROTOTYPES

FROM RENAULT FT TO SEMOVENTE L3

In the final months of the First World War, the Italian army, which had developed a keen interest in armoured vehicles, purchased four Renault FT tanks from France: two with cast Girod turrets (1 MG, 1 gun) and two with riveted Omnibus turrets (both fitted with MGs). The Italians at first seemed intent only on producing a simple copy, but soon began modifying and improving on the existing FT design, a process that would eventually lead to what was perhaps the best tank of the early 1920s, the FIAT 3000.

After the end of the war, in 1919, two of the four Renault, FT tanks purchased by France were sent to Libya, while the other two were used for training activities.

One of these tanks, which was dismantled at Ansaldo's factory, was partly reassembled and converted into a self-propelled gun, known as the Semovente da 105/14. and this turned out to be the first Italian vehicle to adopt the name 'self-propelled'.

In order to develop the idea of using the existing FT chassis for a self-propelled gun, the version with the armed Girod gun FT No. 66947 was selected for the complex prototype work. The project was led by engineer Bennicelli and was realised by Ansaldo. In fact, it was a simple conversion: the turret was removed and in its place a 105/14 mod. 1917 mm howitzer was installed, facing backwards, inside an open combat chamber. It was soon realised that the cramped space of the vehicle had no room for ammunition, which therefore had to be transported separately, which obviously severely limited its tactical usability (at least until a subsidiary, also tracked vehicle was made available to travel alongside, i.e. an FT refuelling variant).

Finally in April 1919, the prototype of the first Semovente 105/14 was ready and was shown, in the presence of the King, Victor Emmanuel III, at the Stadio di Roma. The Italian army at the time planned to order 12 Semoventi 105/14, but nothing came of it and the planned order was never realised.

This vehicle eventually found itself assigned to the Batteria Autonoma Carri d'Assalto, based in Turin, later transferred to Nettuno, near Rome, and as mentioned took part in the parade at the Rome Stadium in April of the same year.

The 105/14 howitzer mounted by this first Italian self-propelled gun was originally called 'Obice da 105 Campale', which after the nomenclature reform of 1926 simply became 'Obice da 105/14'.

▲ Rare image of the Semovente da 105/14 on a modified Renault FT light tank. Wikipedia CC1.

It was used by the artillery of the Royal Army until the end of World War II. Produced towards the end of the First World War, it was only distributed to the units in the run-up to the Second World War.

It was never very successful and ended up being used mainly in fixed locations.

This curious self-propelled vehicle derived from the Renault FT was actually put into production. In the end, the resulting tank remained too archaic and modest a platform, and the general staff thought it was better to leave the vehicle as it was or use it as a tractor. In 1919, the time was probably not yet ripe, and so this FT too was no more than a curious experiment. A sort of test bench to test the idea while other vehicles were being developed that were more suitable.

However, the arrangement of the cannon, mounted facing backwards in relation to the direction of travel of the vehicle, remains unusual. The arrangement of the peculiar curved spade at the rear, designed to overcome trenches, makes the whole thing look rather sci-fi. Finally, the very small, and exposed, space available to the artillerymen in charge of firing should be noted.

What can I say about a self-propelled vehicle, which, for a first, certainly did not lack originality.

▲ Another sharper image of the Semovente da 105/14 on a modified Renault FT light tank (Wikipedia CC1). In the two small photos, two moments of the presentation of the new army vehicles in Rome, the famous Fiat 2000 can also be seen.

SEMOVENTE MOTO GUZZI 65/17

THE GUZZI SEMOVENTE

Northern Italy, with its mountainous and treacherous landscape, was hostile terrain and unsuitable for the use of tanks. However, the mountains offered significant defensive advantages, and an army capable of deploying small armoured vehicles, combined with mobile artillery, would have gained a significant strategic advantage.

With the evolution of military doctrine in the late 1920s, which placed increasing emphasis on tactical and strategic mobility, Italy was faced with the need to develop a vehicle capable of meeting both requirements: light weight and artillery capability. Early approaches were devised with the study of British vehicles such as the Carden-Loyd Mark VI and Mark V. These vehicles presented insights and ideas, such as small size and good mobility, but also significant limitations due to the cumbersomeness of the vehicles.

Moto Guzzi engineers go into action

The Società Anonima Moto Guzzi, best known for the production of motorbikes, contributed to military development with innovative ideas. The company designed an armoured motorbike armed with a heavy machine gun, but above all distinguished itself with a daring design: a fully tracked vehicle in two versions. The first served as an experimental tractor, while the second was armed with a machine gun.

Both versions of the Moto Guzzi project shared the same basic structure. The vehicle consisted of two independent tracked units, mounted on movable arms and connected to a front engine. Behind the engine were the driver and another crew member, responsible for driving and any maintenance. The test bench had a safety cabin, probably designed to protect the crew during a rollover. However, it is unclear whether this feature would be retained

▲ The good 65/27 mountain gun, used here by Alpine troops during the Great War, was the weapon of choice for this bizarre self-propelled gun designed by the historic Mandello del Lario company.

in the final version of the self-propelled vehicle. The vehicle's suspension was an extremely innovative design for the time. Each caterpillar operated independently, thanks to a four-wheel system mounted on a support bar, with an idler pinion and a transmission toothed wheel. This system, supported by three rotating arms, allowed the vehicle to maintain a stable position even on rough terrain or side slopes of up to 45 degrees. It was an unprecedented solution in Italy and the world, ideal for mountain combat requirements. A tactical idea that Italy had dedicated itself to after the tragic experiences of the Great War.

■ TECHNICAL FEATURES

Engine and power supply

Moto Guzzi had already demonstrated expertise in the design of compact and powerful engines, but it is not known which power unit was used in the prototype. At the front of the test bench was an unidentified cylindrical component, which may have been an exhaust or a fuel tank. It is likely that the configuration would have been modified in the final version of the vehicle.

Armament

In its configuration as a tractor, the vehicle was intended to tow light cannons, while in the self-propelled version it was to mount the reliable 65 mm mountain cannon Mod. 1913. Produced by the Royal Arsenal in Naples, this weapon was ideal for combat in mountainous environments thanks to its ability to be disassembled into five parts for easy transport. The cannon used high explosive and shrapnel ammunition, with perforating and hollow charge variants developed later.

Conclusion

The Moto Guzzi Semovente Moto Guzzi project was an avant-garde idea, perfectly suited to the needs of mountain combat and designed to make the most of the mobility and technical characteristics of the 65 mm cannon. However, the initiative was discontinued in 1930, leaving Italy without a concrete solution for an armed vehicle intended for such special scenarios. The Moto Guzzi projects were shelved, and the Regio Esercito was forced to look elsewhere for a suitable vehicle for its needs. All the study and design ended up in a single prototype.

▲ Pictures of the various tests to which Moto Guzzi subjected its self-propelled tank project in the 1920s.

SEMOVENTE MOTO GUZZI 65/17

▲ Semovente 65/17, Moto Guzzi prototype 1921-1930.

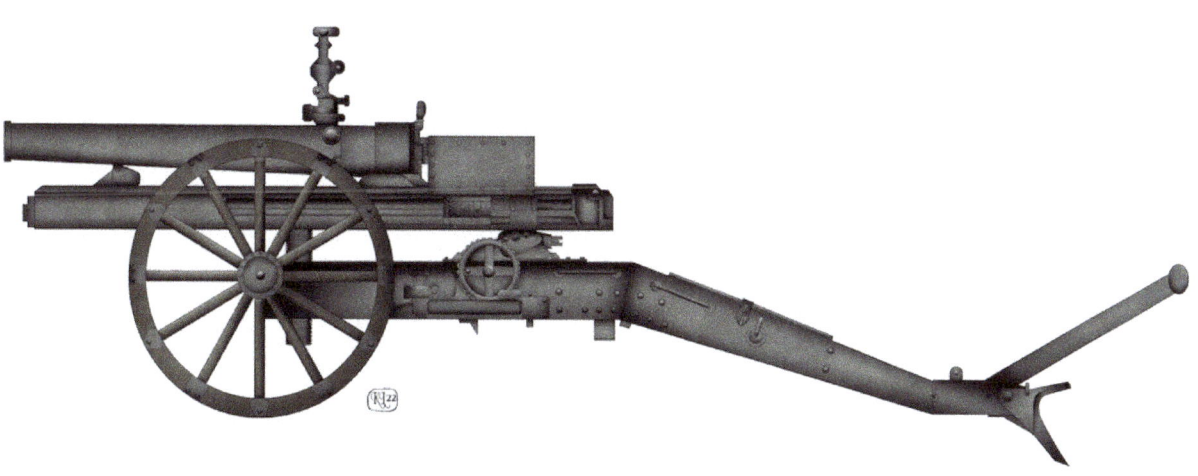

▲ 65/17 gun for Alpine troops - used in the years 1915-1945.

ANSALDO 9 TON SEMOVENTE

▲ Ansaldo 9-tonne self-propelled tank, Italy 1929.

▲ Interesting picture showing the Ansaldo assault/semovente tank next to an M11/39 tank.

ANSALDO 9 TON SEMOVENTE

In 1929 Ansaldo made contact with Foster & Co. Lincoln in Britain to design a turretless tank. The 1:10 scale prototype was then presented in Italy, it was designated 'Carro Armato Ansaldo 9t' and fitted with a 65 mm cannon in the casemate. The vehicle, developed under British supervision in years when the two nations still remembered that they had been allies during the Great War, was built for Italy and tested one last time in 1935, shortly before the invasion of Abyssinia.

The vehicle, built in 1932 and initially named '9t M.33 tank', was tested at length by the CSM until December 1934, but was still unsatisfactory at that date due to its low speed of only 22.5 km/h.

To improve performance, a new engine, spring suspension and modifications to the side armour plates to compensate for the additional weight were introduced between 1935 and 1937.

The original, narrow, square casemate was redesigned to enlarge the interior space: the rectangular front plate was replaced with a trapezoidal one, adding triangular sections on the sides and improving ergonomics and protection. The new, wider configuration increased practicality in the use of the gun and improved defence against machine guns. These modifications required years of work, during which the design evolved to adapt to changing military requirements.

▪ TECHNICAL FEATURES

The design of the 9-tonne tank was relatively simple, almost odern, but concealed some noteworthy features. The basic structure was that of a large wedge with a steep front and a small upright nose that connected to a wide sloping glacis. Above the vehicle was a casemate that formed a combat compartment closed on four sides and equipped with a roof, which protruded beyond the track line. The casemate narrowed at the front and then gradually widened towards the rear. The width of the rear was slightly greater than that of the front hull.

▲ In the side view, the relatively low profile (also compared to the tank at the side) of the Ansaldo 9-tonne tank design is evident, as are the characteristic armoured side plates above the suspension. The wide wing is only interrupted by the large stowage box, which is located approximately in the middle of the tank's length. Source: Ansaldo.

Behind the casemate, the structure descended towards the rear of the tank with a small step starting at the roof. The sloping section narrowed slightly at the top before widening again to the width of the hull. In this space at the rear of the casemate were a number of gun mounts, which, thanks to the sloping configuration, allowed complete coverage with the machine gun at the rear of the tank. The structure was of the type entirely bolted internally to a steel frame, instead of being riveted, as was the case with British tanks of the First World War. However, the bolts could be loosened to allow the plates to be removed when necessary. On each side of the hull were two full-length tracks with suspensions located behind side armoured plates that covered the full height of the tank. A British-patented mud chute system was included, which prevented the accumulation of debris inside the tracks. Although the tracks were exposed all the way around, there was no specific protection to prevent mud from accumulating on the top of the tank, although the projecting sides of the casemate offered partial protection. The 9t tank relied on the projecting sides of the casemate to reduce mud accumulation, although mud could still seep into the rear grilles and drains.

Exhaust gases were expelled through openings on the port and starboard sides of the rear of the hull and then directed outwards, thus preventing smoke from contaminating the crew quarters. The casemate was equipped with a large rectangular hatch sliding to the rear, while on the port and starboard sides were two large rectangular access hatches, opening forward and equipped with ball mounts for machine guns. The front of the casemate housed the main armament, with a ball mount for a machine gun, another larger one for a cannon, and a small rectangular hatch for the driver, located on the lower left. Following the trials, the casemate underwent modifications that enlarged its dimensions and changed its shape.

▲ The original front design, with three vertical columns of bolts, was particularly narrow. When the rectangular casemate front was replaced with a trapezoidal plate, which allowed the battle chamber to be enlarged, a fourth row of bolts became necessary. Source: Ansaldo

▲ The Ansaldo assault tank, surrounded by military personnel and mechanics. The photo was probably taken during the evaluations at Sciarborasca. The difference in the structure of the new casemate is evident by comparing the two pictures: the original shown on the previous page and the new, wider version shown above. Another relevant aspect is the weight of the vehicle. In 1938, the tank project managers at Ansaldo published a document to clarify the criteria for classifying tanks according to weight. Light tanks were defined as those of 5 tonnes or less, while 'assault tanks', intended to penetrate enemy lines, should weigh between 6 and 8 tonnes. Heavy tanks, on the other hand, had to have armour of at least 40 mm, weighing between 14 and 15 tonnes and being smaller in size.

Engine

The internal configuration of the vehicle is perhaps the most interesting aspect of the design. Unlike traditional designs, in which the hull was manufactured separately (welded, bolted or riveted) and then fitted with the engine and gearbox, this vehicle integrated all the components into a single system. Two long steel beams ran the inside length of the hull, starting at the front, where the driver's seat was located.

The driver manoeuvred the vehicle using a pair of brake levers, two pedals, and a dual control for the gearbox, which adjusted the engine speed and transmission.

The engine was positioned in-line, immediately behind the driver and attached directly to this frame, connecting to the mechanical transmission and final drives located at the rear. The entire system was firmly anchored to the frame, allowing, with the removal of the rear upper armour plates, the entire mechanical block to be theoretically extracted as a single unit. This approach, in modern terms, is reminiscent of the 'powerpack' concept used in main battle tanks (MBTs), where the engine and transmission are removed as a single module to simplify and speed maintenance.

Although this solution is common today, it was a highly innovative idea in the 1930s. A similar concept would be taken up by the British parent company's team during work on TOG tanks in 1940, but otherwise remained uncommon until the post-war period. Initially, the vehicle was fitted with an 85 hp V6 Carraro engine, but this proved insufficient during testing. Compared to the CV33, the famous light and fast tank capable of reaching 40 km/h, this car would lag behind, leading to the demand for mechanical upgrades. In 1935, when the tank was presented at the Fiera Campionaria in Milan, the engine had been replaced with a FIAT 355 or 355C, both with 6 in-line cylinders and already used in the FIAT 634N trucks. These engines developed 75 and 80 hp respectively, improving the overall performance of the vehicle.

▲ A nice picture of the automotive structure of the tank, with the final drives, the transmission at the rear, the engine in the centre and the steering controls at the front. Source: Ansaldo.

▲ A nice picture of the tank with the original casemate, as seen through the access hatch on the left side. This provides a clear view of the main gun breech, as well as the battle space. Source: Ansaldo.

▲ Some pictures of the tests carried out at Ansaldo's facilities, with the vehicle engaged in climbing a vertical step about 1 m high. Source: Ansaldo.

ITALIAN SEMOVENTI WWII

Crew

The tank required a crew of at least two people. The driver, positioned at the front left of the vehicle, was responsible for driving and operated from a low position. His visibility was limited frontally, provided by a rectangular hatch that could be opened or, under combat conditions, closed and operated through a viewing slot. There were no other slits on the sides of the casemate to allow additional views for the driver, who therefore had to rely on the commander or other crew members for additional information. In addition to the main slot in the driver's hatch, another, smaller one was located above the front machine gun mount, while further vision slots were arranged in the casemate at the other spherical mounts, with the exception of the main gun.

The second crew member was the operator of the main cannon, located on the right side of the cabin. To safely handle the cannon breech or to facilitate loading, the operator could move slightly to the left, positioning himself approximately in the centre of the casemate. The main cannon was equipped with an optical sighting system located to the left of the spherical mount, which allowed the optics to be moved along with the cannon to facilitate accuracy.

There was probably also a third crew member present, who was in charge of operating the front gun. However, it is unclear who was the leader, whether this third man or the operator of the main gun. Considering the limited visibility of the driver, who only had three small vision slots, it is more likely that the role of commander belonged to the cannon operator, who had a larger optical system.

The ammunition carrier was located on the front right, next to the driver, below and in front of the gun breech. This position would have made loading inconvenient for the commander; therefore, it is likely that the second man acted as a loader when he was not engaged with the machine guns. In static positions, ammunition could be passed to the gunner by the driver himself.

The tank leader, whoever he was, did not have any specific optical devices on the roof to improve his view of the surrounding area. He could observe laterally through the vision slits in the spherical machine gun mounts and frontally through the gun telescope or the vision slits. If necessary, although at some risk in combat, he could also observe through the roof hatch, but in doing so he would not be able to manoeuvre any of the tank's weapons.

The only known photograph of the tank with a crew shows two men, which seems to confirm that the vehicle was designed to operate with a crew of only two.

Armament

Firepower was a crucial aspect of this tank's design, as its breakthrough role required the ability to neutralise both defensive positions and enemy infantry.

Protection against infantry was provided by five spherical machine-gun mounts: one positioned in the upper left part of the casemate, two mounted on the side doors and another two located in the rear part of the superstructure. Unlike other Italian tanks of the time, this vehicle did not have machine guns mounted on the roof. The absence of a turret meant that it was necessary to use the rear mounts or, alternatively, to remove a machine gun from the front or side mounts and operate it manually through the roof hatch to cover the rear of the vehicle.

The sloping sides of the casemate allowed the spherical mounts a limited angle of fire, up to 45 degrees to the front and sides, with a reduced coverage capacity at the rear. The main gun's ammunition rack was located in the front right-hand side of the hull, next to the driver, and was tilted upwards to facilitate access to the bullets. With a capacity of 35 rounds, the ammunition rack was made of shielded metal to protect the bullets from shrapnel, but did not include protective flaps for the shells at the rear.

Analysing the interior of the original casemate, it is evident why it was later enlarged: there was insufficient space to allow easy rotation of the main gun to the left, where the breech was obstructed by the side wall. At the same time, the left front gun was restricted in its movement to the right. The rear of the casemate, under the crew seats, offered space for the storage of additional ammunition boxes.

A total capacity of 80 rounds for the main gun and about 3,000 rounds for the machine guns was also estimated. However, these numbers are probably based on an analysis of the available space and storage options.

SEMOVENTE L3 47/32

The small 47/32 Semovente, derived from the famous L3 light tank, represented the first Italian attempt to develop a tank destroyer by mounting the versatile 47 mm model 47/32 cannon on an armoured vehicle.

It was developed during the interwar period to provide Italian assault infantry units with a light and mobile vehicle. This Semovente was equipped with the standard cannon used by the Italian infantry divisions of the time. The official request arose in 1939, after the Great Exercises of the year XVII EF, from General Fidenzo Dall'Ora, commander of the Armoured Corps, who referred to the installation of the 47/32 Model 1935 cannon on a self-propelled vehicle with armour resistant to machine gun fire.

On 12 August 1939, a prototype of a self-propelled gun on an L3/35 hull, armed with a 47/32 cannon, was presented to the Centro Studi Motorizzazione.

Designed shortly before the Italian side entered the war, the new vehicle used the L3/35 light tank chassis. The choice of weapon fell on the 47/32 cannon (the famous elephantine), which was mounted at the front of the vehicle, while the crew compartment was forced open to accommodate the weapon, given the vehicle's small surface area. Initially, the gun was completely exposed, making the crew vulnerable to small arms fire. To remedy this problem, a protective shield was added, and the prototype was completed. However, the vehicle was deemed too small to effectively carry the 47mm cannon, and the project was abandoned.

In its place, the 47/32 L40 self-propelled tank (see below), based on the L6/40 light tank, was preferred.

The impression one gets from looking at the Ansaldo images of the Semovente L3 is that it would have been an excellent tank destroyer in the Italian technological tradition!

Although this vehicle never got beyond the prototype stage, it seemed to deserve a place in the roll of honour of indigenous Italian vehicles.

▲ Side view of the Semovente L3 47/32 at the Ansaldo workshops. Photo by Ansaldo, colouring by the author.

TECHNICAL FEATURES

The hull and battle chamber
The 47/32 Semovente was based on the chassis of the 3-tonne Light Tank Model 1935. To accommodate the gun, the original casemate was completely removed, and a folding shield was also installed to provide protection for the crew against small arms fire and shrapnel.

Armour
The armouring of the chassis was identical to that of the light tank. The front was 14 mm thick, while the sides and rear were protected by 8 mm plates. The engine compartment was covered with even lighter 7.5 mm plates, while the vehicle floor had 14 mm protection.
The cannon shield was designed to be dismantled and stowed on the sides of the vehicle while on the move, as it restricted the pilot's view.
Once the operational position was reached, it was reassembled. In fact, this feature was not at all practical, and was indeed very inconvenient and dangerous, as removing the shield completely reduced the protection of the L3. It must also be said that the shield mainly protected the engine, adding a thickness of 10 mm on the front and an additional 5-6 mm on the sloping sides.

Engine and suspension
The self-propelled vehicle was fitted with a FIAT Tipo CV 3-005 petrol engine, the same as the one used by its 'parent' the aforementioned L3/35 Tank. It was equipped with a four-speed gearbox and a reverse gear. The ignition was via a crank, which could be used both from inside and outside the vehicle.
The suspension was modified to withstand the weight and recoil of the 47/32 cannon. This improvement is visible in the pictures of the prototype, as is the small window for the pilot's view, located on the left of the shield.
To address the frequent track breakage problems that historically plagued all L3 models, the 47/32 Self-propelled was equipped with an improved suspension system. Each bogie was equipped with a special coil spring, and the tracks were composed of 72 short, single links made of pressed steel, designed for greater reliability and strength.
The vehicle also had two fuel tanks of 40.5 litres each, located on either side of the engine, above the mudguards. This configuration ensured a range on the road of about 7 hours, more than the 5 hours of the L3/35, thanks to the low weight of the self-propelled vehicle, which was about 150 kg less than the light tank.
The theoretical maximum road speed was 38 km/h.

DATA SHEET SEMOVENTE L3 47/32	
Producer	Ansaldo Fossati - Fiat
Length	3660 mm
Width	1410 mm
Height	1500 mm (also considering the gun's shield)
Release/retirement date	1939
Weight	3.300 kg
Crew	2 (pilot and gunner/cannoneer)
Engine	Type CV 3-005 petrol 42 hp
Maximum speed	38 km/h on road, 14 km off road
Autonomy	7 hours on the road
Fuel tank capacity	2 tanks of 40.5 litres each
Produced quantity	few prototypes
Maximum slope	60%
Frontal armour	14 mm front and ground, 10 mm gun shield
Side armour	8 mm side and rear
Engine compartment armour	7,5 mm
Armament	1 gun 47/32 Model 35 (53 shots)

SEMOVENTE L3 47-32

▲ 47-32 self-propelled vehicle not used in wartime, only prototype 1942.

▲ 47-32 self-propelled not used in wartime, only prototype 1942.

Armament

The vehicle was equipped with the 47/32 Model 1935 cannon, originally developed in Austria by Böhler in 1935 and later produced under licence in Italy and the Netherlands. In the Regio Esercito this weapon was used both as an infantry support gun and as an anti-tank gun, earning it the affectionate nickname of *Elefantino* among the soldiers.

Initially, the cannon was mounted on a pedestal at the front of the vehicle, but soon after the first tests a protective shield was added to defend the crew from enemy shrapnel and bullets.

The cannon could be oriented with a lateral inclination of 15° on each side and enjoy an elevation ranging from -18° to +30°.

Ammunition

The 47/32 self-propelled gun could carry up to 53 47 mm projectiles, stored in a metal case at the rear of the driver's cab. Although no detailed information is available on the types of ammunition stowed, the gun was compatible with a variety of projectiles, including anti-tank and fragmentation rounds (see next pages).

Crew

The crew of the L3 Semovente L3 consisted of two people: a gunner/cannoneer and a driver.

However, initial tests revealed a significant vulnerability: crew members were exposed and inadequately protected, even against light fire, making them vulnerable to artillery and air attacks. This was also one of the main reasons for the vehicle's lack of success.

The small size of the vehicle did not allow the addition of additional self-defence weapons, such as an anti-aircraft machine gun, or an increase in the number of crew members. This limitation forced the gunner to also take on the role of commander, having to perform several tasks at once: observing the battlefield, identifying targets, aiming the cannon, firing and giving orders to the pilot.

In addition to driving, the pilot was also responsible for reloading the cannon when the vehicle was stationary,

▲ Front view of the 47/32 L3 self-propelled gun. Photo by Ansaldo, colouring by the author.

▲ The famous 47/32 anti-tank and infantry support gun, friendly called 'elefantino' by the Italian soldiers. Model preserved at the Rocca historical museum in upper Bergamo (photo by the author).

▲ Three-quarter view of the same 47/32 L3 self-propelled gun. Photo by Ansaldo, colouring by the author.

but if engaged in driving, the commander also had to take care of this operation.

This greatly reduced the rate of fire and compromised the efficiency of the vehicle in combat.

Operational use

The 47/32 Semovente on Hull L3 never entered production. It was submitted for evaluation on 12 August 1939 at the Centro Studi della Motorizzazione (Motorisation Study Centre), and subsequently presented to Benito Mussolini on 26 October 1939. On the same day, General Alberto Pariani, Chief of Staff of the Regio Esercito, wrote to General Manera to express his appreciation for the project, considering it suitable for the intended role. He suggested, however, the addition of a Breda machine gun for anti-aircraft defence.

Manera in turn proposed to order as many as 300 units of the vehicle, on the condition that production would start immediately and all the required modifications would be made. However, by 21 October 1940, the project was officially halted. The decision was taken during a meeting between General Mario Roatta, Deputy Chief of Staff, and General Mario Caracciolo di Feroleto, Senior Inspector of Technical Services.

The two opted for the development of a new self-propelled vehicle armed with a 75 mm cannon, inspired by the German Sturmgeschütz III (StuG III), and in the immediate aftermath the L40 tank self-propelled vehicle, which offered better crew defence. In short, new, more advanced designs were preferred, consequently leading to the final abandonment of the 47/32 L3 self-propelled vehicle.

In the spring of 1941, the only prototype of the Self-propelled L3 was still kept at the Motor Vehicle Research Centre, but there is no certain information about its subsequent fate, and its trail has been lost ever since.

Ammunition for 47/32 Model 1935 gun					
Name	Type	Initial speed (m/s)	Ammunition weight (kg)	Penetration (mm)	
				500 m	750 m
Grenade Cartoccio Model 1935	High explosive	250	2.860	//	//
Perforating Grenade Model 1935	Armour piercing	630	2.035	25	//
Perforating Grenade Model 1939	Armour piercing	630	2.055	40	35

▲ Structure of the experimental installation of the 47/32 Model 1935 gun on the L3 hull.

▲ Side view with operators at the L3 47/32 self-propelled gun piece. Photo by Ansaldo, colouring by the author.

▲ Various types of grenades for the 47/32 gun. Wiki CC1.

SEMOVENTE B1 BIS (FRANCE)

▲ French Char B1 bis tank self-propelled captured by Axis forces, 1940.

▲ In 1940, with the fall of France, the Germans and Italians proceeded to occupy the transalpine nation. Part of the nation, after agreements with the Germans became Vichy France. In the areas occupied by the Italians, a number of factories and industries were located and in some of them the Italian army tracked down Char B1 Bis tanks. The vehicles were almost complete and several of them were without turrets, but the Italians decided to test them anyway, renaming them 'Semovente B1 bis', but the time proved to be monstrously long and by mid-1943, the vehicle ended its test period in the Italian ranks. In view of the situation that was now unfolding, the tank was left to its own devices.

SEMOVENTE L40 47/32

The L40 47/32 self-propelled tank was used in a number of units by the Italian army and later, after the armistice, also by the German army; it was a conversion of the L 6/40 light tank in order to be able to install an Italian 47 mm anti-tank gun.

During the Second World War, Italy did not distinguish itself with significant achievements in the design of armoured vehicles. However, by the end of the 1930s, the Italian army was at least theoretically competitive with other countries in the field of self-propelled anti-tank vehicles. To confirm this, the industry developed the L3 47/32 self-propelled vehicle project, which we have already discussed in the previous chapter. This was a vehicle armed with a 47 mm anti-tank cannon (the elephantine), equipped with a 32-calibre barrel. This gun was mounted on a gun carriage at the front of a low, compact hull, derived from the famous L.3 fast tank, with a two-man crew. However, the design was unsuccessful, as the vehicle was in fact weak and provided no protection for the operators.

When Italy entered the war in 1940, it became evident that the country's much-vaunted armed forces were equipped with very inadequate means in terms of both armament and protection. The situation was particularly critical for light tanks, which had received a large part of the available funding.

Of these, the L 6 series had significant flaws: poor protection and a 37 mm cannon, which was too weak for an effective anti-tank role. The L 6/40 tank proved to be completely ineffective against British vehicles deployed in North Africa, which forced the General Staff to consider the possibility of developing a self-propelled anti-tank vehicle, with limited swing, using the same hull. The design was entrusted to a collaboration between Fiat SPA and Ansaldo.

The new self-propelled vehicle, called the L40 47/32, was armed with an Italian version of the Austrian Böhler 47 mm cannon, a dual-purpose weapon, effective both as a counter-tank and for infantry support, considered among the best of its era. This cannon was installed on a simple casemate structure, mounted directly on the hull of the tank.

Although the design was basic and the vertical walls of the superstructure were not sloping to provide greater

▲ Rare example of the L4 self-propelled vehicle preserved in the American Museum at Fort Lee. Wikipedia CC1.

SEMOVENTE L40 47-32

▲ Semovente 47-32 employed in wartime operations in the Cyrenaean desert. Libya, 1942.

▲ Semovente 47-32 used during the last containment campaign in Tunisia, 1942.

protection, the vehicle still represented an improvement over its predecessors. Entering service in 1942, 280 examples were produced. The self-propelled vehicle proved quite effective against lighter British tanks in the fighting in North Africa, being able to carry up to 70 rounds on board.

The Ansaldo Semovente was later built by FIAT between 1942 and 1944. It was designed primarily to enable the Bersaglieri regiments, famous assault infantry units of the Royal Italian Army, to provide direct fire support from the 47/32 Mod. 1935 cannon, without having to tow it as had always been the case before, and secondly, to provide Italian armoured divisions with a vehicle with anti-tank performance.

This vehicle was used from 1942 to 1945 by Italy and Germany, as well as the Independent State of Croatia and the Yugoslav partisans who captured several examples. In total, 402 vehicles were built in different variants. After the Italian armistice of September 1943, the German forces in particular took advantage of this by requisitioning, along with many other R.E. vehicles, numerous L40 47/32 self-propelled vehicles and integrated them into their operational units in Italy.

However, the mountainous terrain of the peninsula, where most of the fighting took place during the Allied advance northwards between 1944 and April 1945, was hardly suitable for the use of armoured vehicles. For this reason, many self-propelled vehicles were deprived of their main cannon and converted into mobile command vehicles, equipped with 8 mm Breda Model 38 machine guns, which were much more useful.

Despite being a relatively simple design, the L.40 47/32 self-propelled gun represented concrete proof of Italy's ability to understand and develop the concept of self-propelled anti-tank vehicles early in the conflict. During the first phase of the project and during testing, continuous improvements were made.

During tests at the end of 1940, it soon became apparent that the limited space of the combat chamber hindered the tasks of the three crew members assigned to the vehicle; therefore, it was ordered that the roof of the vehicle be removed, decreasing the protection of the crew but increasing the space available.

An interesting and strange curiosity is the presence of the access hatch on the right side. Both the prototypes and the first series vehicles were equipped with it, inherited from the L6/40. The hatch could never be used because there was a rack in front and, consequently, it was welded to the structure, in short a pseudo-hatch.

DATA SHEET SEMOVENTE L40 47/32	
Producer	Ansaldo Fossati - Fiat
Length	3820 mm
Width	1920 mm
Height	1630 mm
Release/retirement date	1940-1945
Weight	6.825 kg
Crew	2/3
Engine	SPA 18D 4-cylinder 4053 cm^3 petrol engine
Power	70 hp (52 kW) 4053 cylinder capacity
Traction	Tracks
Maximum speed	43 km/h on road, 16 km/h off road
Autonomy	200 km
Fuel tank capacity	165 L
Radio	RF1 CA
Maximum slope	60%
Frontal armour	30 mm
Side armour	15mm
Rear armour	15mm
Armament	1 gun 47/32 Mod. 38 of 47 mm. 1 8 mm Breda Mod. 38

▶ L6/40 ammunition carrier version. The vehicle was designed to supply the 90/53 Semovente heavy fighters. The vehicle could carry 26 projectiles of 90 mm calibre and a further 40 projectiles could be transported in the ammunition trailer. Thirty of these vehicles were produced, one for each tank destroyer..

▲ Top view of the L4 self-propelled vehicle hull. Fiat photos.

SEMOVENTE L40 47-32

▲ Semovente L 47-32, 3rd Company of Gruppo Corazzato "Leonessa" GNR RSI. Italy, April 1945.

▲ Semovente 47-32 used in Sicily in July 1943.

TECHNICAL FEATURES

Engine and suspension

The 47/32 Self-propelled L40 had the same engine as the L6/40: the FIAT-SPA 18D petrol-driven, 4-cylinder, liquid-cooled engine with a power output of 68 hp (70 hp according to some sources) at 2,500 rpm and a volume of 4,053 cm³. It could be started electrically or manually, used a Zenith 42 TTVP carburettor and required different oils according to temperature (ultra-thick above 30°C, thick between 10°C and 30°C, semi-dense below 10°C). The oil had to be changed every 100 hours or 2,000 km. The 165-litre tanks guaranteed a range of 200 km on the road and 5 hours off-road, with maximum speeds of 42 km/h and 20-25 km/h respectively.

The bogie included a front cogwheel, four coupled drive wheels, three upper rollers and a rear idler wheel on each side. The swing arms were fixed to the chassis and connected to torsion bars, a novelty for Italian vehicles. The tracks, with 88 links per side, were derived from the L3 series.

Armour

The armour of the L40 was also similar to that of the L6/40: 30 mm for the front plates, 40 mm for the gun shield and driver's door, 15 mm for side and rear plates, 6 mm for the engine deck and 10 mm for the floor. Made of low-quality steel, (like most Italian armoured vehicles) the armour was vulnerable to cracks even against non-penetrating small-calibre shots.

The bolted plates, although dangerous for the crew (the bolts could detach and be shot into the cockpit at great speed), made the vehicle easier to manufacture and allowed for quick field replacements, a necessity for Italian industry at the time.

Hull and interior

At the front, the transmission cover included a driver-operated inspection hatch, often left open to cool the brakes. A shovel and crowbar were mounted on the right wing, while the left wing had a jack stand. For night driving, a single headlamp was mounted on the right, as the left one had been removed for the 47 mm gun shield. The driver, positioned on the right, had an opening slit and an episcope with a field of vision of 30° horizontal, 8° vertical, and tilt from -1° to +18°. It had the gear lever and hand brake on the left, and the dashboard on the right. Magneti Marelli batteries were located under the seat and powered the engine and electrical systems. Behind the driver, a box contained a spare episcope and a bullet holder for 33 rounds, above which was the magazine. To the left, an armoured bullet holder for 37 rounds occupied almost all the little space available. The fighting compartment was crossed centrally by the drive

▲ L40 Ammunition carrier for 90/53 self-propelled vehicle, Sicilian campaign, 1943.

shaft. The gunner/commander, positioned on the left, had the cannon breech in front of him with cranks for horizontal and vertical movement. To the right of the cannon was the 1x optical sight, manufactured by San Giorgio di Sestri-Ponente, also used on the 'M' series tanks.

The small interior space did not allow for an intercom system. On the sides of the superstructure were rails used to secure the sun and rain cover, facilitate access to the vehicle and carry backpacks, helmets or spare tracks for additional protection.

Armament

The 47/32 Semovente L40 was armed with the Mod. 1935 47/32 Cannon, also known by the nickname 'Elefantino'. Designed by Böhler and produced under licence in over 3,200 units between 1937 and 1945 by companies such as Breda, ARET, AREP and Ansaldo, it was a very reliable and accurate gun, effective up to 4,000 m for infantry support and 1,000 m for anti-tank fire, with a maximum range of 7,000 m. Mounted on the left side of the hull, it had a horizontal rotation of 27° and vertical rotation from -12° to +20°.

Despite the small space, the crew often carried light weapons for close defence, such as Carcano Mod. 91 rifles, MAB 38 machine guns and OTO, Breda or SRCM Mod. 35 grenades, stowed in boxes or bags on the engine deck.

Ammunition

The cannon had 70 rounds and fired five types of ammunition. The rate of fire was about 15 rounds per minute, but in enemy fire situations the magazine, reduced to passing bullets to the gunner, slowed the rate of fire. The limited availability of HEAT ammunition, which was introduced late, was a significant problem. In May 1942, there were only 12,537 out of a total of 145,777 47-mm EP rounds in North Africa.

Mod. 35 armour-piercing ammunition had an estimated penetration of 37 mm at 700 m. The Mod. 39, on the other hand, penetrated 55 mm at 100 m, 40 mm at 500 m and 30 mm at 1,000 m, at an angle of 0°.

▲ The interior of the prototype. You can see the bolt holes on the superstructure where the armoured roof was fixed. From this picture you can clearly see the cramped space inside the casemate.

Campuflage and markings

During the Second World War, Italian L40 47/32 self-propelled vehicles were initially painted in light khaki (Saharan). Those deployed in the Soviet Union were instead painted olive green between the summer and winter of 1942, while retaining some traces of the original colour, a scheme used only on the Eastern Front, even in winter. In North Africa, Italy and France, camouflage remained the standard khaki, sometimes supplemented with foliage to reduce visibility to air attacks. In the field, crews added Italian flags, mottos and new camouflage patterns.

With Allied air dominance in North Africa, the L40s were increasingly camouflaged with nets and vegetation, a practice maintained during the 1943 campaign in Sicily. The markings identified the vehicle, company and platoon: an Arabic number for the vehicle, a coloured rectangle (red, blue or yellow depending on the company) and vertical white lines for the platoon. Command vehicles had rectangles divided into two or three colours, depending on the companies, with an 'R' to indicate the presence of radios.

Under the Italian Social Republic, camouflage schemes varied. The 'Benito Mussolini' Bersaglieri Battalion added olive green stripes, while the 'San Giusto' Squadron Group used non-military paints to apply brown and dark green stripes or tricolour camouflage. Finally, the 'Leonessa' Armoured Group kept the khaki colour, adding fascist symbols such as the red 'm' and the fascio littorio. Some vehicles were repainted with Continental camouflage.

Conclusions

The L40 self-propelled gun, armed with a 47 mm cannon, proved to be rather ineffective against the more modern British, American and Soviet tanks by the end of 1942. Primarily designed for close support of Italian assault units, it proved very effective as an infantry support vehicle due to its ability to hit targets up to 4,000 metres with good accuracy.

Its main shortcomings included a lack of secondary armament and radios, insufficient armour and very limited interior space.

These shortcomings were partly resolved in the third series produced for the Germans after November 1943, but the size of the vehicle never allowed it to be equipped with more powerful armament appropriate to the times.

▲ Semovente L6/40 being landed in Libya at the beginning of the conflict. State Archives (author colouring).

SEMOVENTE 75/18

INTRODUCTION

The 75/18 self-propelled tank belonged to the family of Italian tank destroyers, designed precisely to support medium tanks that, alone, were unable to counter the opponent's vehicles.

The vehicles were all based on the medium tank chassis in different variants: M13/40, M14/41 and M15/42. The first version, the best known, was armed with an Ansaldo 75 mm L/18 cannon placed in the casemate. The 75/18 and its later version, 75/34, were able to fight on equal terms against almost all enemy armoured vehicles during the Second World War.

As proof of the good product, it must be remembered that even the Wehrmacht, usually not very tender in its 'unofficial' judgments on our vehicles, found the self-propelled vehicle very well made, so much so that after 8 September, it was the Italian vehicle they used the most. As mentioned, its versatility allowed the *Regio Esercito* its use in various fields, but especially in the support of infantry, tank fighters and the M40 and 41 medium tank. In total, between 225 and 360 vehicles were produced in the various versions. The serious and full-bodied reasons referred to the need for the Italian army to have at its disposal armoured vehicles capable of countering those of its adversaries, the British and Russians.

DEVELOPMENT

Design began by Ansaldo-Fossati in 1938, the year after the M40 medium tank was launched. The designer was Giuseppe Rosini. At first, a 47mm cannon was considered, but military experience soon changed the mind and the choice fell on the more powerful 75/18 howitzer Mod. 1934, already known as an excellent artillery piece. It was decided to use the hull of the M40 medium tanks, and later the M41 and M42. The choice of the 75-calibre was also prompted by the good experience hitherto provided by German tank destroyers equipped with a similar gun. The father of the gun project was Sergio Berlese, a colonel in the *Artillery Technical Service* (STA), who worked in collaboration with Ansaldo engineers. Already in mid-1941, after witnessing the effectiveness of the vehicle in comparative tests, the self-propelled gun was immediately ordered and put into production. Nevertheless, the first vehicles only reached North Africa in 1942. Moreover, despite its good results, the vehicle was not produced in sufficient numbers, due to an archaic idea within the General Staff that considered a 'double' artillery, albeit mechanised, to be almost useless. By the time it was seen that the 75/18

▲ M40 self-propelled tank with 75/18 gun in the Ansaldo workshops in Genoa. This is one of the first examples produced by the Ligurian company. State Archives.

was the only means, or almost the only means, capable of countering the adversary's means, it was too late, with the revolution of the assembly lines only occurring in 1943, when for Italy the fates were already decided.

As mentioned, the vehicle, apart from its armament and rigid casemate arrangement, inherited the same technical characteristics as its parent vehicle, the M tank. The crew in this case, however, was reduced to three men: the driver, as in the M tank, was positioned at the front, on the left side, with the loader behind him; the tank commander sat on the right side and had to deal with aiming and firing the cannon as well as giving orders to the crew; finally, the loader also acted as a radio operator/marshaller.

■ ARMAMENT OF SEMOVENTE

The main armament, as mentioned, was the 75/18 gun. A half-track armed with the 75/34 piece was also under consideration, but remained in the planning stage until 1942/43, when it too saw the light of day. The cannon was centrally located at the front of the casemate and housed on a pivoting ball mount, which allowed the gun a good angle of movement both vertically and horizontally, compensating at least in part for the lack of a movable turret. The 75/18 artillery piece was quite modern and had long been supplied to the army in its field version. In the case of the self-propelled , it was equipped at the apex with a muzzle brake with small burst holes. The magazine provided inside each vehicle consisted of 41 rounds. Although this cannon had a low initial speed, it could fire at a range of 9 km in the field version and slightly less in the self-propelled version.

Put to work, the 75/18 soon proved to be a highly effective weapon that claimed many victims among its many tanks of the calibre of American vehicles such as the M3 Grants, M4 Sherman or the British Mk VIII Cromwell: M3 Grants, M4 Sherman or the British Mk VIII Cromwell.

▲ The 75/18 mod. 35 howitzer, shown here in the artillery version, was a valuable and modern piece. Samur Museum (France).

SEMOVENTE M40/41 75/18

▲ Prototype of the self-propelled 75/18 M.40 at the Ansaldo factories in Genoa, Italy 1941.

▲ Semovente 47-32 used in Sicily in July 1943.

The 75/18 self-propelled tank also acted as mobile artillery, providing indirect supporting fire to the assaulting infantry battalions. As secondary armament, like the medium tanks, the self-propelled vehicle also had a Breda Mod. 38 machine gun. This could also be used as an anti-aircraft gun, which was often the case, as to avoid complications caused by smoke filling the casemate inside the self-propelled vehicle even after only a few shots had been fired, it was a healthy habit to leave the doors open on the vehicle's overhead.

■ PRODUCTION

The first prototype of the self-propelled 75/18 saw the light of day in February 1941. It was mounted on the M40 hull and 30 examples were immediately ordered. On 30 April, the first vehicles were delivered to the 133rd Armoured Division 'Littorio' and the 133rd Artillery Regiment. Each delivery group consisted of two batteries of four self-propelled vehicles for a total of eight self-propelled vehicles, four command tanks and a reserve of two self-propelled vehicles and one command tank. A few months later, at the beginning of 1942, the vehicles were embarked for the African war front and here reassigned to the 132nd Regiment of the 132nd Armoured Division 'Aries', which was located in El-Agheila.

In Libya, the self-propelled vehicles had their baptism of fire in the spring of 1942 and remained active throughout until the defeat suffered at El Alamein in November of the same year. From the very first battles in the desert against enemy forces, it was realised that the self-propelled vehicles did not have an adequate amount of ammunition on board.

To make up for this, the self-propelled vehicles were accompanied by Saharan trucks adapted for the extra transport of ammunition for the 75/18. While suitable trailers such as the Bianchi truck, the Lancia Ro or the Viberti trailer were used for transport over long distances. In June 1942, it was then decided to mount the self-propelled vehicle on the newly improved M14/41 hull.

This new production went to supply units for the 'Littorio' and 'Ariete' divisions and the 131st Armoured Division 'Centauro'. Numbered DLI to DLXI, all operational and deployed in Libya and Tunisia, due to adverse

▲ Picture of the gun breech inside the casemate. Photo by the author (Militaria Novegro 2022).

▲ Various details of the 75/18 M14/41 self-propelled gun exhibited at the Militaria fair in Novegro. On the left, the breech, the pilot's seat and the shape of the 'cartridge box' below the gun can be seen; on the right, the lubrication tanks and control organs of the self-propelled vehicle. Below on the left one can see the radio apparatus and a tank driver's helmet, on the right the pilot's seat.

fortunes, they ended up being destroyed for the most part despite achieving various successes. Only those remaining in Italy were saved. Subsequently, the third version was introduced, the one mounted on the M15/42 hull, which went on to equip the new units including the 'Lancieri di Vittorio Emanuele II' Regiment of the reborn 'Ariete' Division. The 75/18 was later joined by the very last 75/34 self-propelled vehicles. Another tank battalion equipped with the new M42s was assigned to the 12th Infantry Division 'Sassari', which flanked the Ariete armoured division on 9 September in an attempt to bar the Germans' way to Rome. After the armistice, most, if not all, of these vehicles were handed over to the Germans. The only 75/18 self-propelled vehicles that remained in Italian hands were the M42s of the DLXI Group that remained in Sardinia, but due to the continued mistrust of the Allies, these vehicles remained virtually non-operational.

TECHNICAL FEATURES

The tank consisted of the chassis or hull, the armament, the engine and its transmission, locomotion and control components. Its mass varied, depending on the model, between 13 and 14 tonnes. It was 4.9 to 5.06 metres long, 2.28 metres wide and 1.85 metres high including the periscope.

These are the main parts: hull - accesses - inspection hatches - exhaust holes - visibility means - engine - transmission organs - steering and braking organs - external propulsion organs and suspension.

Hull: consisted of special steel plates (forming the armour plating) rigidly connected on the inside by a strong framework of sections and reinforced by crossbeams, so as to obtain a watertight case resistant to the most violent stresses and shocks.

The lower part of the hull was watertight, which allowed it to ford torrents.

The armour plates were of different thicknesses and were distributed in such a way as to ensure maximum protection for the parts most exposed to fire. Inside, the hull was divided into two parts by a vertical bulkhead to form an engine chamber at the rear and a combat chamber at the front. The engine chamber contained, in addition to the engine with fans and radiators, the two fuel tanks and accumulator batteries. The combat chamber comprised the central part and the front part of the hull; in it were contained all the tank's steering and

▲ Interior of the fighting casemate. Note the black-coloured peephole at the back. Photo by the author.

transmission components.

The 'low' combat casemate, a good 50 mm thick, housed the three-man crew, the ammunition bonnets and shelves, the radio station, the personal weapons, the Breda mod. 30 and its ammunition. The roof of the combat chamber had two lids/exit vents that opened outwards. On the top of the turret was a support for the installation of the machine gun for firing and anti-aircraft defence, while on the left side of the roof was the support for the antenna of the transceiver station and, on the right side, that for the panoramic telescope intended for the exploration of the surrounding terrain. The electrical system differed from that of the M tanks in that it had a single battery pack, located on the engine chamber and comprising four Magneti Marelli 3NF-12-1-24 type batteries; each had a voltage of 6 volts and were connected in series. However, the hull incorporated some modifications, such as air filters and new silencers.

Access: a double one in the turret for the entire crew. The roof hatch, divided in two, could be kept open by means of two props.

Inspection hatches: two on the engine chamber and two at the brakes. The two engine bonnet hatches were attached to a central hinge. They were closed from the outside by means of two pins with wing nuts; from the inside by means of a safety catch. The two front doors for inspecting the brakes could only be opened from inside the tank, by means of a device controlled by hand by the driver. This device made it possible to keep the doors partially open during travel for cooling the brakes.

Visibility from inside the tank: for driving, the driver had a rectangular slot cut in the front plate of the casemate, with a hinged hatch on the outside and operated with a lever from the inside. The hatch could assume a fully open position -remaining almost horizontal- and all other intermediate positions until fully closed.

With the hatch closed, direct visibility was possible through a longitudinal slit in the hatch, which could be closed from the inside by means of a plate fixed to the hatch and operated with a special pin.

The pilot's eyes were protected from shrapnel by a crystal contained in a box attached to the plate and easily removable.

In addition to direct visibility, the pilot had at his dispos-

▲ Interior of the casemate. In view the seats occupied by the pilot and servant, on the left the instrument bench. Photo by the author.

al, for guidance, a means of indirect visibility consisting of a hyposcope. This apparatus, which allowed the tank to be steered when it was necessary to keep the driving hatch closed during combat, was essentially composed of two prisms, an upper one -objective- protruding from the roof of the hull, and a lower one -ocular- placed in the interior at the pilot's eye level. For rear and lateral visibility, the foreman and the porter faced the outside of the casemate with the hatches open. No slits were provided apart from two minute circular ones protected by pivoting plates located on either side of the rear wall. However, a periscope and other sights were available for the head-tanker.

Engine: fast, four-stroke, diesel type; 8 cylinders in a block -four on each side- arranged at 90°, V-position. This type of engine differed fundamentally from the normal internal-combustion engine in that the fuelling and ignition took place in a completely different way.

Unlike normal internal combustion engines, fuel injection engines had no fuel to prepare the mixture of air and petrol outside the cylinder. In this engine, the intake into the cylinder was done directly from the atmosphere; only a filter was inserted at the end of the intake duct to trap any impurities and dust contained in the air. At the end of the suction, only air was introduced into the cylinder, on which normal pressure was exerted during the upward stroke of the piston.

The fuel for injection into the cylinders was supplied by special injection pumps, one per cylinder, grouped in a single mechanical unit, controlled by a suitable transmission from the engine. Ignition of the injected fuel took place automatically (except for the first cold engine start, which was facilitated by the spark plugs, which were powered by a current of 2 volts). This was followed by the normal bursting phase and then the exhaust phase, the final phase of the operating cycle, which was renewed in full, as in all normal four-stroke internal combustion engines. From the M41 version onwards, the interior of the self-propelled aircraft was adapted to accommodate the SPA 15T injection engine to replace the 8T, which powered the M13/40.

Starting the engine:

1) *Hand-operated* from both inside and outside the tank, by means of a hand-crank-operated inertia starter fitted

▲ Image of the self-propelled 75/18 M14-41. Photo by the author (Militaria Novegro 2022).

with a push-button.

2) *Electric*, by means of two starter motors acting on a gear wheel attached to the flywheel.

Lubrication: oil circulation was by means of three pumps, two of which were recovery and one delivery. The scavenge pumps drew oil from the two sumps in the engine sump and sent it to the sump.

Cooling: was by forced water circulation using a centrifugal pump. The pump was driven by a double chain and a sprocket on the crankshaft. Water cooling was achieved by fans blowing air through the two radiators.

Air filters: There were four of them, attached to the engine, two on each side; they consisted of a wire mesh winding in which a filter of special fabric was housed. Their task was to filter the air before it entered the cylinders during the intake phase.

Transmission-clutch parts: incorporated in the engine flywheel, it consisted of: a clutch control housing; a pressure plate ring; a driven disc invested in the clutch shaft; twelve springs. The clutch was released by depressing the pedal; this, with special rods and levers, controlled the clutch release sleeve, which in turn caused the pressure plate to move away, compressing the springs more.

Transmission: The drive shaft was used to transmit the movement of the drive shaft to the gearbox and planetary unit located at the front of the tank. The shaft was protected by a tube and protective cover and fitted with universal joints.

Gearbox: the gearbox was of the sliding block type, with gears always meshing and direct drive. Three shafts: primary, subsidiary, secondary and a reverse shaft.

In the box, separated by a wall, was the speed reducer, which allowed a reduction to the normal gears. Thus, one had four normal and four reduced gears. A special lever was used to engage this reduction and directly connect the secondary gearbox shaft with the axle, i.e. the truncated cone and planetary assembly.

Direction and braking organs: they were part of a planetary complex, which was designed to allow: a) transmission of motion to the wheels; b) direction; c) braking.

Two direction levers, located on either side of the driver, were placed on the left to control the tank steering. Manoeuvring these levers caused the braking of the tracks and consequently the steering of the tank, which pivoted on the braked track.

Braking of the tank: slowing down and stopping the tank was achieved by simultaneously acting on the two direction levers; for stronger braking, the brake pedal was pressed at the same time, which therefore functioned solely as an intensifier of the braking action.

External propulsion and suspension parts - Drive wheels: placed on the sides of the hull at the front, they received motion from the drive shafts. These consisted of a wheel with two flanges to which two toothed rings were attached for transmitting motion to the crawler. Also attached to the inner flanges of the wheels were toothed crowns with pinions that received motion from the drive shafts and protruded from the front circular openings of the hull.

Tracks: each track consisted of 8 equal links hinged together by means of pins, the slipping out of which was prevented, on the one hand, by a stop in the hole of the last hinge and, on the other, by a stop pad embedded in a groove in the links. In the centre of each link was a guide flap and, at the sides of this flap, two rectangular holes into which the drive wheel teeth were inserted.

Idler wheels and idler units: The two tracks, which relied on the drive wheels at the front, rested on two idler wheels at the rear, the pivots of which were carried by longitudinally movable idler arms. The displacement caused the tension to increase or the track to loosen.

Guide rollers: each track was guided and rested its upper branch on three rubberised rollers, rotating on pivots fixed to the sides of the hull.

Suspension: the tank, through the pivots of four plates nailed to the sides of the hull, rested elastically on four bogies, two on each side. The bogies, each consisting of two pairs of rubberised rollers, were located on the sides of the hull, so that the load was evenly distributed on each of them. Each bogie was independent of the others and had the ability to swing around the pivot of the corresponding plate. The elastic system, made up of springs, levers and rocker arms, not only ensured the elastic suspension of the bogie, but also allowed the bogie to deform so that the track could adapt to any unevenness in the terrain and keep constantly in contact with the bogie rollers. This eliminated one of the main causes of skidding.

Armour plating: the type of construction and materials used in Italian tanks were not up to the standard of foreign production, especially with regard to the chemical composition of the armour plates.

The armour plating was also bolted on (an Italian

characteristic in WW2 armoured vehicles), not cast. The armour often tended to split in the event of a collision with an enemy projectile, even if there was no penetration, because it was too 'rigid', malleable and poorly treated. The armour reached a maximum of 50mm at the front of the casemate and a minimum of 14mm at the bottom of the hull.

Interior arrangement: the engine could be started either electrically or by hand by means of an inertia starter, which could be operated both outside and inside the vehicle.

The tank was equipped with an electrical system that provided external lighting (with two lights on the sides of the casemate and a single light at the rear) and internal lighting with two bulbs on the dashboard and two in the *fighting chamber*.

The system, of course, also provided engine starting.

The elevation, and the cannon's swing, were controlled by hand by means of two steering wheels to the left of the gunner/head gunner. All the optical instruments on board were built by the San Giorgio company.

Radio system: the radio system, which was almost completely absent in the first tanks produced, consisted of an 'RF1 CA' type set. positioned on the right side of the hull.

A telegraph was not fitted for internal communications, as was the case with the M tanks, because, lacking the turret, the three men were all at the same height and in a cramped space they communicated directly.

Source: S.M.R.E. - '*Nozioni di armi, tiro e materiali vari*', Edizioni Le 'Forze Armate', Rome, 1942.

Concluding remarks

British technicians from the Tank Technology School in Cobham examined a 75/18 M40 self-propelled gun captured in Africa and wrote a flattering report, although it did not mention the effectiveness of the armament. In objective terms, the British praised the mechanics, describing them as efficient and practical, especially the suspension and steering. The 8T engine, although underpowered, was considered very compact and easy to access. The only criticism was levelled at the armour, which they considered to be below acceptable standards for the Allies, and they complained both about the lack of splinter protection and the exposure of the suspension, which was particularly vulnerable to anti-tank mines.

▲ Self-propelled version on M.13-40 hull (recognisable by the partial wing). Saumur Museum - Wikipedia.

VERSIONS OF THE VEHICLE

As was already the case with the medium tanks, three main versions were produced from their derivatives for the Regio Esercito, including definitive operatives and prototypes. The most important ones are listed below.

- *75/18 M13/40*: first designation of the self-propelled vehicle, designed by Ansaldo in 1938. This first version was produced in only 60 examples, in two stages. The armament was mainly based on the 75/18 mod. 1935 cannon and Breda mod. 30 machine gun on board the vehicle. The M13/40 was powered by a liquid-cooled, 8-cylinder SPA 8T diesel engine. The associated gearbox had 4 forward gears and a normal reverse gear; in addition, thanks to the built-in gearbox, a further 4 gears plus an additional reverse gear were available. The engine of choice was one of the tank's major handicaps: it was underpowered and prone to various failures, due to sand and a deplorable lack of filters. It weighed 13 tonnes, had a maximum speed of 33 km/h and a range of 215 km.

- *75/18 M14/41*: the successor model to the first was produced in 162 examples (some speak of 300) and equipped with the new 145 hp Fiat SPA 15T V-8 diesel engine. The vehicle was almost identical to its predecessor, both in mechanics and armament. The hull differed only in the shape of the track covers extended along the entire length of the tank and other small details. The new engine also brought new radiator grilles, with fins oriented parallel to the major axis of the tank. A mud-hunting lever for the drive wheel was introduced, as well as other improvements to the electrical system. The armament and its layout were also identical. In addition to the combat tanks, several radio control tanks were also produced. It weighed 13.5 tonnes, so a little heavier than its predecessor. Thanks to the new engine, it enjoyed a slightly higher speed of 35 km/h.

- *75/18 M15/42*: produced in an uncertain but rather low number, it was the third and final general improvement in every respect, but considering the time, it came too late to be able to face the new enemy tanks on an equal footing. Due to the ensuing events of the Cassibile armistice of 3 September, production was soon

▲ M14-41 Command Tank (Archive P. Crippa. Author's colouring).

▲ Column of 75/18 self-propelled vehicles in North Africa around 1942. Note in the front row a command tank with two twin machine guns derived from the M40 medium tank. State Archives. In the small photo: the march of the self-propelled vehicles in the Libyan desert.

discontinued. The last model in the series was delivered in May 1943. The number of units delivered to the Regio Esercito was, as mentioned, only 60, while the others ended up being used by the Germans (who put it back into production) and the regular army of the Italian Social Republic. The main differences with the previous versions were: a greater length of the vehicle at the rear of about 15cm; and the placement of the spare wheels on the bottom of the tank. After 8 September 1943, as mentioned, the Germans took possession of all Italian self-propelled vehicles (except those in Sardinia). They then ordered the new production of 75/18 and 75/34, which were delivered in 1944. The weight was now 15 tonnes, with improved protection, and a length increased by about 15 cm. Speed, thanks to a third new engine, was now 39 km(h). It also had smoke grenade launchers carried in a box at the rear of the hull.

The tanks used by the Germans were renamed *StuG M42 mit 75/34 (851)*, all of which were regularly equipped with an RF1 CA radio and immediately distributed to the armoured detachments of the German army.

BASED ON SEMOVENTI 75/18

- **75/34 M15/42**: Another version of the self-propelled cannon was the 75/34 on an M.42 hull, preceded by a prototype armed with a 75/32 Mod. 1937 that was not fully convincing. The improved and later produced version had a 75/34 Mod. SF gun with a longer barrel and more powerful ammunition, which greatly increased anti-tank performance. Ordered in 253 units, only sixty were produced and delivered to large armoured units in August 1943. The new cannon allowed for a very interesting range: 12,000 metres. The initial speed was also significantly increased.

- *M.40, M.41 and M.42 command tanks*: together with the 75/18 self-propelled tank, a command tank variant was developed on the orders of the General Staff. It was basically a normal medium-sized tank without a turret and equipped with the necessary equipment for battery firing direction and radio links. The turret compartment, initially enclosed, had an upper access with the same two hatches as the original tank. During series production, however, a total of four hatches were created, allowing more space for observers. The combat chamber housed the crew of four: on the left was the pilot and on the right

▲ Two pictures of the self-propelled 75/34 M.15-42 with the new, longer and more powerful barrel (State Archives).

the gunner, on the two rear seats were the commander and the goniometer. The gunner was in charge of the two 8 mm Breda 38s on the M40, which were replaced by a single 13.2 mm Breda Mod. 31 in the later versions; the compartment also housed another 8 mm Breda machine gun with a special wolf's mouth mount for anti-aircraft fire. Finally, inside the vehicle were the ammunition, optical equipment, control instruments and steering gear. On the upper and rear ends of the right side of the roof were the mounts for the two radio transmitter antennas. The panoramic telescope was located on the left corner of the roof. Produced in a total of 139 units, they were mainly used to direct the fire of self-propelled artillery guns. Two Magneti Marelli radios, one RF1 CA and one RF2 CA, and two extra batteries were placed in the casemate, and a rangefinder was installed.

A curiosity: a signal gun with 45 rounds was stored inside the vehicle. Each battery consisted of eight self-propelled guns and two command tanks.

- **M14/41 Radio Tank**: in addition to the standard Magneti Marelli RF1 CA radio, it was equipped with an RF2 CA. The antennas were mounted on the left side of the hull and, by means of a knob, it was possible to lower them from inside the combat chamber to allow rotation of the turret on that side. This craft, if intended for airborne communication, was eventually also equipped with the RF3M radio. This had a longer signal range than the RF2CA radio device. Thirty-four M14/41CRs were produced and two were distributed to each battalion command.

▲ A self-propelled 75/18 hit and knocked out of action by British armoured personnel carriers in the African desert. (Wikipedia. Author colouring). Small photo: a broken-down self-propelled vehicle is being towed for repairs.

SEMOVENTE M13 40 75/18

▲ Semovente 75-18 on an M.40. hull belonging to the 5th self-propelled group, 132nd Artillery Regiment of the Division Armoured Aries, at El Alamein, Egypt, August 1942. Note the Breda mod. 30 on the roof of the vehicle at the disposal of the tank leader.

▲ Semovente Command Tank 75-18 on M.40 belonging to the Ariete Armoured Division, in Cyrenaica, February 1942.

ITALIAN SEMOVENTI WWII

▲ After the armistice of 8 September 1943, (in the small photo: a self-propelled vehicle in the area of Porta San Paolo) conducted in a very clumsy way by the Italian General Staff, the Germans, with their usual organisation and timeliness, quickly put the disbanded Italian army out of action and seized and reused much of the war material that had already belonged to the Royal Army. In the photo you can see a considerable amount of equipment, mainly medium-sized and self-propelled tanks in German hands (Arena Archive).

OPERATIONAL USE

As soon as the first 75/18 self-propelled vehicles were produced, they were delivered to the Armoured Divisions mainly as divisional mobile artillery units. Only in the field did it become clear, however, that their most decisive use would be as tank fighters, as at the time medium tanks were poorly suited to stopping enemy armoured vehicles, such as the British Matilda and the Crusader, but later also US tanks such as the M3 Lee and M4 Sherman. The self-propelled vehicles were distributed in two groups for each armoured division, which in turn consisted of two batteries of four self-propelled 75/18 tanks each, four command tanks for each artillery group and a further two self-propelled and one reserve command tank, making a total of 18 self-propelled and 9 command tanks. Production of the M40 version consisted of only 60 vehicles divided into 6 groups indicated by Roman numerals from DLI to DLVI.

◼ BAPTISM OF FIRE IN NORTH AFRICA

The two groups formed in 1941 carried out their training in Italy in two phases: the first concerning the use of artillery and the second the use of armoured vehicles, before being sent into combat in North Africa. The best experience, however, was the desert war, where, despite the well-known deficits of the Regio Esercito, the use of self-propelled vehicles was highly successful, especially during the second Italian-German offensive, which started from El-Agheila in January 1942, after which there was a reorganisation of the units according to the new requirements. The first two batteries delivered were the IV and VI, (Group DLI) and were assigned to the 'Ariete' (132ª Armoured Division) on 14 May 1942. These first two were later joined by the DLII Group in the same division. Later, a new group, the DLIV, was ready, which went on to arm the *131st Armoured Division 'Centaur'*. Finally, the two groups DLV and DLVI, went to the *133rd Armoured Division 'Littorio'*. All the personnel of the self-propelled vehicle crews were from artillery and not tank crews as on the M tanks. The operational life of the 75/18 self-propelled vehicles began towards the end of 1941, lasting until the end of the war. The most intensive employment was certainly in North Africa in the ranks of the three Italian armoured divisions 'Ariete', 'Littorio' and 'Centauro', until the surrender in Tunisia in

▲ Line of self-propelled vehicles deployed in the Cyrenaean desert, 1941. State Archives (author colouring).

May 1943. But already at El Alamein, most of the DLI, DLII, DLIV and DLVI groups were all but destroyed. However, as mentioned, prior to El Alamein, the General Staff of the Italian forces in Libya expressed a very flattering opinion on the use of armoured artillery: *'The self-propelled 75/18 gave excellent proof of itself, combining single shot power with better technical requirements and better manoeuvrability than the M-tank'*. Consequently, the War Ministry decided to place an order for 163 new M42s, but these entered service too late, in May 1943. The swan song of the self-propelled vehicles took place at El Alamein, the oft-mentioned great battle of the desert. Here, two armoured groups of self-propelled vehicles were engaged, the DLIV and DLVI, with a total of 35 vehicles. For the occasion, they were equipped with more than double the usual range of more than a hundred rounds per self-propelled unit. Placed around the heights number 33 and 34, they almost all perished except for two that managed to return. Twelve other vehicles belonging to the DLI and DLII groups, also of the 'Ariete', placed at the rear of the front line, tried in every way to stem the impetuous British advance, inflicting considerable losses on the enemy (according to Italian sources, 30 enemy tanks, including Sherman, Grant and Crusader). In contrast, the 'Ariete' was totally destroyed. The two survivors mentioned were also lost shortly afterwards in the defence of the Ridotta Capuzzo. At the beginning of 1943, the Italians succeeded in organising the new 'Centaur' division sent to Africa from Greece. This division made up of veterans was also the only one that succeeded against the North American forces in Africa. Their greatest success, in fact, was the Battle of Kasserine in February 1943.

■ ITALY, SICILY

After the loss of Africa, the few self-propelled vehicles that could be saved, along with those stationed on the peninsula, were framed in the following armoured divisions: the *135th Armoured Division 'Ariete II'*, which counted 94 M41 75/18 among its ranks (divided between the *Armoured Exploring Regiment* and the *Armoured Regiments*). Other self-propelled vehicles were employed by the *Armoured Motorized Regiment* stationed in Sardinia, which did not actually take part in any combat during World War II, and whose vehicles were the only ones not to fall into German hands after the armistice. Other self-propelled vehicles were combined with the *XII Anti-tank Group* of the *'Sassari' Infantry Division* and the six squadrons belonging to the *'Lancieri di Vittorio Emanuele II' Regiment*.

Their first commitment was the defence of Sicily following the Allied landings in July 1943. After the loss of Sicily, Italy decisively matured its exit from the conflict by agreeing to sign the Cassibile Accords in Sicily.

Then, until the armistice of 8 September, and before the tragic events of the defence of Rome, the self-propelled 75/18 had no particular war commitments to report.

■ ITALY, ROME, SEPTEMBER 1943

From 8 to 10 September, the 'Ariete II' was involved in clashes against the Germans in and around Rome,

▲ Self-propelled tanks in the Libyan desert in 1942, from the magazine *Cronache di Guerra* (author collection).

SEMOVENTE M13/14 40-41 75/18

▲ Self-propelled 75/18 M.40 2nd Battery 1st Group of the Ariete Armoured Division, on Lancia 3Ro transport. Cyrenaica Desert, Libya, June 1942.

▲ Semovente 75/18 M.41 1st Company, 31st Tank Regiment, 134th Armoured Division Centaur El Guettar, Tunisia, January 1943.

▲ Two pictures of the same M40 self-propelled vehicle loaded onto a Viberti trailer to be transported to the operational area. Note the Breda machine gun mounted on the roof of the vehicle and also the yellow black triangle insignia, typical of self-propelled vehicles in Africa. State Archives. Author's colouring.

particularly at Porta San Paolo. There were also clashes in Cesano, and on the Via Ostiense leading to Rome. But as a result of the poor or non-existent preparation for the defence of the capital, even with more men and means, it ended up that most of the Italian troops withdrew, by superior order, to Tivoli, effectively abandoning the defence of the city. Most of the Regio Esercito's vehicles fell into German hands and went to equip the 2ª *Fallschirmjäger-Division*. The only noteworthy reaction on the Italian side occurred at Porta San Paolo, one of the main entrances to the city of Rome, on 10 September. Here, Italian soldiers of the *21st Infantry Division Grenadiers of Sardinia*, the *I Squadron* of the *'Genoa Cavalry'*, some units of the *'Sassari' Infantry Division*, Paratroopers of the *10th Arditi Parachutisti Regiment* supported by several civilians, including many women, fought heroically and with commitment against the German forces that wanted to enter the city. On that occasion, numerous 75/18 self-propelled units took part in the action, as can be seen from many photos, also published in this book of ours. The resistance, which began at dawn on the 10th, did not end until after 5 p.m., when the remaining Italian forces withdrew, then joined the partisan forces, making sure first to put their vehicles out of action to prevent the Germans from using them again.

■ SELF-PROPELLED VEHICLES PASSED TO THE GERMANS AND THE RSI

After the Italian surrender in September 1943, the occupying German forces used most of the captured vehicles, and among them, the self-propelled ones were the favourite, so much so that production of the 75/18 also resumed with slight modifications. A second spare roll for smoke mortars was added to the rear of the superstructure and the rear of the hull. The new 75/18 and 75/34, together with almost all Ansaldo production vehicles, participated from then on under the German insignia in all the fighting of the Italian campaign until 2 May 1945.

In general, therefore, self-propelled vehicles also shared the fate of all Italian war material that the Germans found useful to redeploy. The 75/18 self-propelled vehicles were repainted with the typical German armoured vehicle colours and were attached to their fighting units.

A few examples were subsequently granted for use to certain units of the National Republican Army of the RSI. Among these, the following were given self-propelled vehicles: the 'San Giusto' Armoured Squadron Group to which, in addition to four M tanks, three 75/18 self-propelled vehicles on M42 hulls and one 75/34 self-

▲ Libyan front: in the foreground a 75/18 M41 and in the background, in a military car, General Erwin Rommel. Bundesarchiv.

▲ Uniform of Italian tank drivers 1940-1945, plates and symbols used on tanks and self-propelled vehicles. Artwork by the author.

SEMOVENTE M14 41-42 75/18

▲ Semovente Command Tank 75/18 M.41 of the 'Piscitelli' Group, Tunisia, March 1943, formerly in the DLVII Group operating in Sicily in January 1943. Self-propelled vehicles in the period were named after old artillery and rifles of the past.

▲ Semovente 75/18 M.42 of the 'Sassari' Infantry Division 13th Battalion, 2nd Company in Rome, Italy, 9 September 1943.

▶ Front view of a 75/34 self-propelled tank of the R.S.I.'s "San Giusto" Armoured Group on the move, autumn 1944. Viziano Archive.

▲ Semovente 75/18 M.41 knocked out in the clashes in Rome in September 1943. Bundesarchiv.

propelled vehicle on M42 hulls were also made available. The Raggruppamento Anti Partigiani (RAP) - Gruppo Esplorante supplemented two 75/18 self-propelled vehicles on an M42 hull, while the armoured group 'Leonessa' deployed two M42-hulled command tanks for its self-propelled battery.

The German divisions that most recycled captured self-propelled vehicles were: those taken in Lazio, which ended up with the 2^a *Fallschirmjäger Division*. All other vehicles available in German-occupied Italian territory, or captured in Albania and the Balkans, were put on a role with the German armoured divisions. Again, many (but not all) vehicles were repainted and fitted with German coats of arms.

Numerically, the Wehrmacht redeployed around 80 newly produced self-propelled vehicles and 36 war surplus captured from the Italians, renaming the vehicle *StuG M42 mit 75/34 (851)*.

"PARTISAN" SEMOVENTI

The story of the armoured cars that ended up in the hands of the partisan forces is curious and interesting. On 18 April 1945, a big general strike broke out in the factories of Turin, as many as 12,000 Fiat workers crossed their arms in protest. Being at war, they stood in defence of the factories, organising trenches, checkpoints and rushing to arm themselves. Everything went smoothly for a few days, but after about a week the Nazi-fascist reaction was announced. The workers therefore thought of using the military vehicles that were being repaired in the Fiat workshops at the time. Specifically, these were two M.42 tanks and a self-propelled 75/18 M.42. These three vehicles proved very useful in the days to come, contributing firstly to the defence of the factories and then to the defence of the important railway junction at Torino Porta Nuova.

In the last days of the war, with Turin effectively liberated by its workers and citizens, a parade was held to celebrate the imminent end of the war.

Naturally, the partisans 'camouflaged' their armoured vehicles with their colours and insignia. Above all, the names and slogans of the resistance played the lion's share. An M42 self-propelled 75/18 was used by the 7th *Autonomous Partisan Division 'Monferrato'* and arrived in Turin on 25 April 1943, for the aforementioned parade through the city centre.

This vehicle was distinguished by the inscriptions on the walls of its hull: '*W LA MONFERRATO*' and '*W STALIN*', while on the driver's window/spionplate of the vehicle was the inscription 'Ali', which was none other than the name of the commander of the partisan unit that one night captured an armoured vehicle of the 'Leonessa' Group without the RSI forces noticing. To this day, it is still unclear whether this story was a myth or a legend created by the partisans. It is interesting to note that the partisan brigade in question was 'autonomous', i.e. it was not linked to any political group, unlike the Garibaldi Partisan Brigades, which consisted of communists, and the Matteotti Partisan Brigades, which grouped mostly socialists, or those of the Popular and Moderate Action Party. This means that the partisans/workers who painted '*W STALIN*' on the hull did so out of caution, in order to avoid friendly fire.

Other 75/18 self-propelled vehicles used by partisans were seen in Milan, Genoa and other northern Italian cities that were liberated from Nazi-Fascist oppression in the days between 24 and 30 April.

CONCLUSIONS

After the war, a total of 62 self-propelled vehicles survived, including 50 M41 75/18 and 12 M42 75/18, which were largely reused by the Italian Army from 1946 to November 1955. They only began to be withdrawn around 1953, when the newer and more powerful M47 Patton arrived from the United States.

In 1955 they were completely withdrawn from service, but remained in reserve until 1965 when most of them were scrapped. 21 of them were repaired by the Turin arsenal between 1945 and 1950. Many of these self-propelled aircraft are now preserved in museums, civic parks or collections in Italy.

The self-propelled 75/18 cannon was one of the few Italian vehicles to stand up to the enemy vehicles for some time, although it was obviously not without serious shortcomings.

Of these, the most interesting to note was the modest amount of ammunition carried, only 44 rounds, which in fact severely limited its combat performance, forcing the use and support of accessory supply vehicles, by their very nature, very vulnerable.

The range and power of the 75/18 gun soon proved to be lacking compared to the Allied self-propelled guns, such as the Priest or Sexton, or the Wespe. Things improved with the new calibre of the later self-propelled guns, but by then it was too late.

Another major problem was the deficient secondary armament, totally lacking a coaxial machine gun, which made the vehicle very vulnerable to infantry attacks.

Further problems stemmed from the low value of the M-hull, its speed, critical suspension, etc.

SEMOVENTE M13 40 75/18

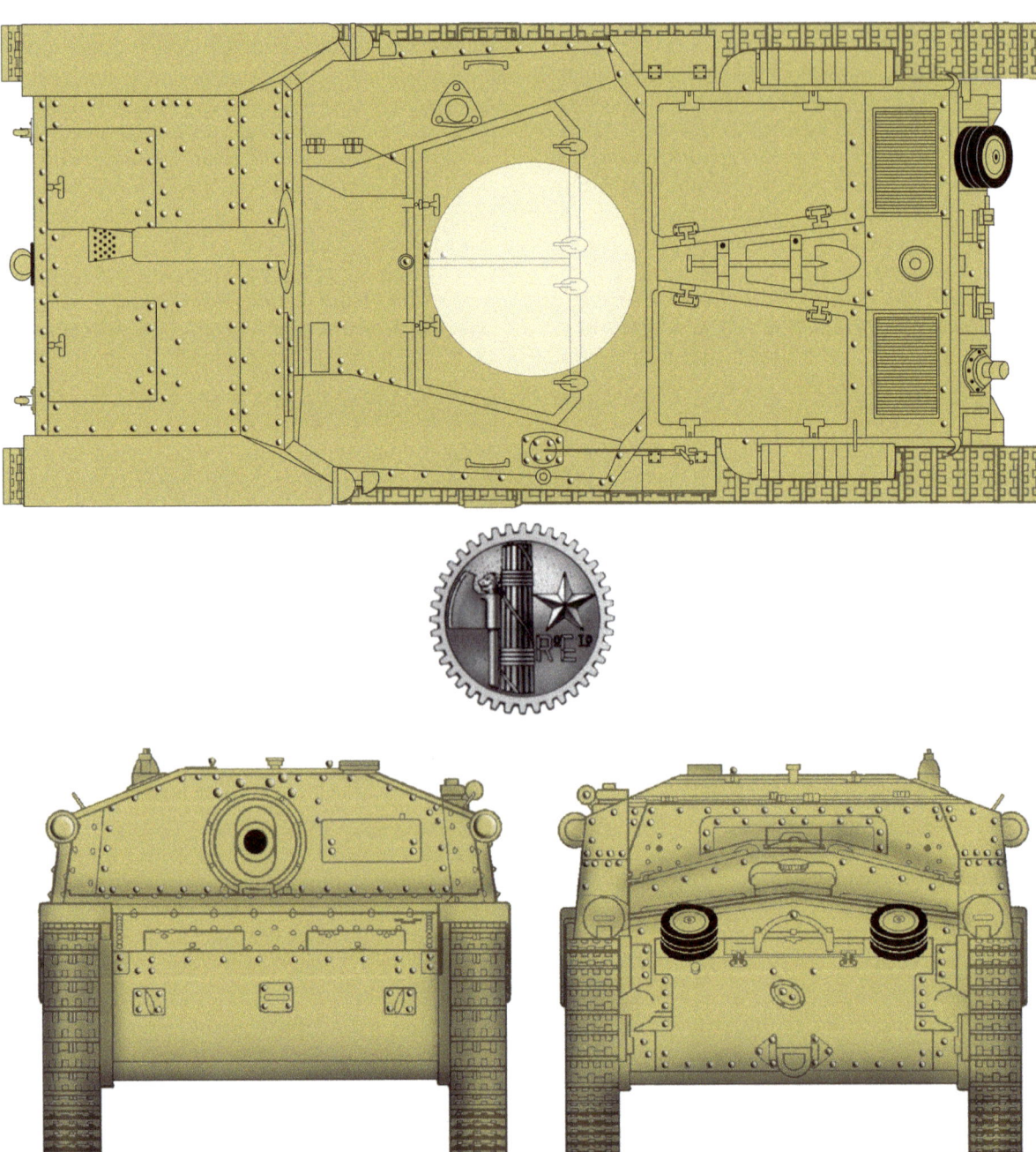

▲ View of the Italian 75/18 M.40 semovente from above, front and rear. Clearly visible on the roof of the casemate is the painted white circle for aerial recognition by friendly aircraft. In small, the bronze or aluminium badge was placed on the top left of the front plate of the armoured vehicles from April 1936 to August 1943.

SEMOVENTE M14 41 75/18

▲ Semovente 75/18 M.41 of the 5th Semoventi Squadron of the 'Lancieri di Montebello' at Porta San Paolo Rome, Italy, 10 September 1943.

▲ Semovente 75/18 M.41 Tank 'Colubrina' of the DLVII Assault Group in Sicily, Italy January 1943. Like the tank of the 'Piscitelli' Group, it too had received an archaic designation.

▲ An Italian 75/34 self-propelled vehicle, already in German hands, has just been captured by British soldiers of the 78th Infantry Division who are examining the vehicle. The British have also already erased the German *Balkenkreuz* and put the battleaxe badge of their division in its place. Italy, May 1944.

PRODUCTION AND EXPORT

Approximately 288 self-propelled vehicles were built by the war, of which 60 M13/40, 162 M14/41 tanks (between self-propelled and command) and a further 66 M 15/42. The number of total vehicles in the different variants, however, is not certain, as the Germans produced their own, and the numbering, mainly for the M41 model, varies widely according to the sources. As production began in wartime, there were no international markets available to which the vehicles could be sold, as was the case with the light tanks, for example. The tanks, mainly due to wartime events, ended up in the hands of the various belligerent and/or allied and former allied nations.

- Royal Army: purchaser and major user of a large part of the production of medium armoured vehicles.
- Australia: following the battles in the North African desert, Australian troops took possession of a number of armoured vehicles, mainly medium tanks, but probably also self-propelled vehicles, which were rehabilitated by the Australians themselves and repainted with typical colours and distinguishing marks (the famous white kangaroos).
- Great Britain: as above, British troops also got their hands on some Italian medium tanks.
- Italian Social Republic: After the collapse of Italy following the events of 8 September, a new state was created in German-controlled northern Italy. The RSI used all the military means of the Royal Army already at its disposal.
- German Army: in the same way, and in a massive and selective manner, the German Army also confiscated and refitted all available Italian vehicles after 8 September. In some cases even reactivating production assembly lines (especially in the case of M15 vehicles and derived self-propelled vehicles).

MAJOR USER

Medium tanks were used by the armies mentioned above, but obviously its main user was Italy and its armoured units: by the Regio Esercito above all, but also, after the Armistice, by the Esercito Nazionale Repubblicano and the Guardia Nazionale Repubblicana, following the establishment of the Italian Social Republic in 1943. A few vehicles were also captured in the European theatres of war, particularly in Dalmatia and the Balkans, captured and reused by the Yugoslav partisans and again by the Greek resistance. Some of these vehicles remained in service in Italy for a short time during the immediate post-war years.

▲▼ Above: self-propelled vehicles in Tunisia in 1943. Below: a self-propelled 75/18 also in Africa.

SEMOVENTE M14/15 41/42 75/18 & 75/34

▲ Semovente 75-34 M.42 3rd Platoon 2nd Company of the 'Lancieri di Vittorio Emanuele II' regiment, part of the Ariete Armoured Division, Rome, September 1943.

▲ Semovente 75/18 M.41 of the Littorio Armoured Division in Italy, 1942.

▲ The crew of an Italian self-propelled vehicle observes the photographer filming them as they pass under the Cestia pyramid in Rome in the September days when Italian troops tried to block the German occupation of the capital.

▼ A self-propelled vehicle put out of action in the September 1943 clashes in Rome (Wikipedia).

SEMOVENTE M14/15 41/42 75/18

▲ Semovente 75/18 M.41 belonging to the DLXI Gruppo Semoventi operating in Sardinia, Italy 1943.

▲ Semovente 75/18 M.42 Panzerjager Abt. 278th Infantry Division, Ancona, Italy 1944.

▲ Various details of the self-propelled 75/18 M.42 preserved at the Parco della Rocca in Bergamo. Photo by the author.

SEMOVENTE M42 75/34

▲ Semovente 75-34 M.42 Italian 'Lancieri di Vittorio Emanuele II' Regiment, operating in the area of the Latium lakes, Italy, summer 1943.

▲ Semovente 75-34 M.42 of the 'S. Giusto' Armoured Group, R.S.I, Italy 1944

▲▼ Towards the end of the war, a few RSI vehicles and a few Germans ended up in the hands of the partisan forces who, in the euphoria of a terrible war that was drawing to a close, painted their mottos and insignia, as in the case of these self-propelled vehicles and light tanks on 'parade' in Turin. (Photo: Paolo Crippa archive).

SEMOVENTE M42 75/34

▲ Semovente 75-34 M.42 in the German army in the Balkans, 1944.

▲ Semovente 75-34 M.42 in the German army on the Gothic Line of the 171st Panzer Divison, Italy, May 1944.

DATA SHEET SEMOVENTI 75/18 & 75/34			
	75/18 M13/40	75/18 M14/41	75/18/34 M15/42
Length	4915 mm	4915 mm	5060 mm
Width	2200 mm	2200 mm	2280 mm
Height	1850 mm	1850 mm	2370 mm
Minimum bottom-hull height from ground	0,38 m	0,38 m	0,41 m
Weight in combat order	13.100 kg	13.500 kg	15.000 kg
Crew	4	4	4
Engine	M 13: Fiat-SPA 8T M.40 8-cylinder V diesel, 11,140 cm^3 M 14: Fiat SPA 15T M.41 8-cylinder V diesel, 11980 cm^3 M 15: FIAT-SPA 15TB M.42 8-cylinder V-cylinder, petrol-powered		
Maximum speed	31,8 km/h on road 13 km/h off road	35 km/h on road 13 km/h off road	39 km/h on road 14 km/h off road
Autonomy	215 km on road 5 h off road	210 km on road 5 h off road	200 km on road 5 h off road
Fuel tank capacity	180 L	180 L	307 L
Armour thickness	From 6 to 50 mm	From 6 to 50 mm	From 6 to 55 mm
Armament	One 75/18 Mod. 1934 howitzer with 44 rounds. 1 Breda Mod. 30 6.5 mm machine gun	One 75/18 Mod. 1934 howitzer with 44 rounds. One 8 mm Breda Mod. 38 machine gun	One 75/18 howitzer and then one 75/34 howitzer. One 8 mm Breda Mod. 38 machine gun

▲ Semovente 75/18 M.41 in the Fossati-Ansaldo workshops. State Archives. (Author's colouring).

THE "ANTI-AIRCRAFT" SEMOVENTE

A very interesting version based on the basic model of the M15/42 tank but equipped with a new polygonal turret obtained by welding, open to the sky, pivoting 360° and containing a quadruple system of 20 mm Scotti-Isotta-Fraschini 20/70 cannons. This was the ingenious self-propelled anti-aircraft gun.

The only other change concerned the removal of the two Breda Mod. 38 machine guns in the casemate, the opening of which was covered by a 42 mm thick plate.

The crew was reduced from four to three men, two in the turret and the pilot in the hull. It was built in a single prototype (perhaps two), which was presented and tested at the Army's Motor Research Centre in early 1943: compared to the original vehicle, the self-propelled anti-aircraft vehicle weighed 14.7 tonnes, and was taller (2.55 metres).

In March, it entered service as 'M15/42 Anti-Aircraft Tank' and was given to the 8th Autieri Regiment stationed at Cecchignola in Rome.

Here, following the armistice, the Germans found and captured it. Of its use, the most credited hypothesis is that it ended up in Austria, where it took part in the fighting and was used until April 1945, where it operated in the Teupitz area, for air defence by the V-SS *Volunteer-Freiwilligen-Gebirgskorps (V-SS* Mountain Armoured Corps), which fought the last battles against the Red Army.

Regarding the hypothesis of the two prototypes, it seems that the second one was transported to Tunisia, where it was tested under real combat conditions.

It remained on African soil after the surrender of the Italian 1st Army and the 5ª *Panzerarmee* in May 1943.

▲ Image of the M15 tank in anti-aircraft conversion. The armament consisted of a quadratic Scotti-Isotta Fraschini 20 mm machine gun system, designed in 1932 by engineer Alfredo Scotti, who later sold the patent (but only for foreign countries) to the Swiss company Oerlikon; the weapon was then developed in Italy by Isotta Fraschini in 1938. The Mod. 1939 version installed on a stanchion mount was used by the Regia Aeronautica for the defence of installations and by the Regia Marina embarked and in fixed installation, even in pairs.

"ANTI-AIRCRAFT" SEMOVENTE

▲ Two pictures of possible profiles of the Semovente M15/42 anti-aircraft vehicle used by the 5th SS Armoured Corps SS Mountain Corps ('*V-SS Volunteer-Freiwilligen-Gebirgskorps*') that fought the last battles against the Red Army.

SEMOVENTE 75/34

INTRODUCTION

We have already partly presented the 75/34 self-propelled gun in a few lines in the first volume dedicated to Italian self-propelled guns. The vehicle, an evolution of the more famous and widespread 75/18, was also a self-propelled assault gun (SPG) produced by Fiat-Ansaldo for the Regio Esercito. The main model of this self-propelled gun was the M42 M, while a few examples of the M43 model were produced towards the end of the war. After the armistice and the subsequent start of the Republican adventure in northern Italy, this vehicle was also adopted, albeit in rather low numbers, by the R.S.I.

DEVELOPMENT

The Regio Esercito had already adopted two self-propelled assault tanks in 1940: the 47/32 L40 self-propelled tank and the 75/18 M41 self-propelled tank for accompanying infantry and as tank destroyers. The latter in particular proved to be the only Italian armoured tank capable of holding its own against the British tanks. Realizing that the 75/18 howitzer was no longer an optimal choice, in June 1941 the Regio Esercito's top management requested an even more powerful self-propelled vehicle from Ansaldo, to which the company responded by proposing the installation of the 75/32 Mod. 1937 gun on the hull of the M41 self-propelled vehicle, itself derived from the M14/41 medium tank. However, this solution did not satisfy the army, which in October 1942 ordered the company's engineers to install the 75/34 Mod. S.F. piece on the hull of the M42 self-propelled vehicle. This second variant satisfied the General Staff and on 29 April 1943, the 'M42 M (modified) 75/34 self-propelled vehicle' was officially adopted and 280 units were ordered.

The first vehicles entered service in May. Before the armistice, just over 90 were built, which went to equip the following army departments:

- The 19th 'M' Tank Battalion of the 1st 'M' Armoured Division: based on 2 self-propelled batteries and 1 M15/42 tank company; each battery was equipped with a Command Self-Propelled Tank and three out of four sections;
- The XXX Counter-Tank Battalion of the 30th 'Sabauda' Infantry Division with 2 companies;
- The CXXXV Counter-Tank Battalion of the 135th Armoured Division 'Aries II' out of 3 companies;
- The 31st Tank Infantry Regiment and the 'Alexandria Cavalry' Regiment (14th).

▲ One of the first images of the prototype of the self-propelled 75/34 in the courtyard of the Ansaldo-Fossati workshops in Sestri Ponente on 26 February 1943. State Archives.

SEMOVENTE M42 75/34

▲ Semovente M42 75-34 belonging to the CXXXV Counter-Tank Battalion of the 135th Armoured Division Ariete II. Cesano di Roma, September 1943.

▲ Semovente M42 75-34 belonging to the CXXXV Counter-Tank Battalion of the 135th Armoured Division Ariete II. Cesano di Roma, September 1943. Picture with Breda and without tanks.

After the armistice, the National Republican Army assigned some of them to the 'San Giusto' armoured squadron group. During the same period, the Wehrmacht also employed 80 newly produced and 36 captured from the Italians, renaming the vehicle StuG M42 mit 75/34 (851) (i). The vehicle was assigned to one company per Panzerjäger Abteilung (tank fighter battalion) of many Heer divisions and to some Luftwaffe Fallschirmjäger units in Italy.

■ TECHNICAL FEATURES

The layout of the new self-propelled vehicle echoes that of its 75/18 predecessors. The M42 hull is derived from the M15/42 tank, of which it retains the rolling train with semi-elliptical leaf spring suspension, the 192 hp Fiat-SPA 15TB petrol engine and the centre-rear section of the hull, without the turret. The front part of the vehicle consists of an armoured casemate made of bolted sheet metal, 50 mm thick on the front section.

Unlike the 75/18, and due to the greater recoil of the new 75/34 gun, the armoured superstructure was lengthened by 11 cm at the front. An easily noticeable detail is the presence of a third bolt on top of the angled front armour plate. The driver sits on the left and has an armoured hatch loophole at his disposal.

In addition to the driver, the casemate housed the gunner leader, who had a periscope at his disposal for (manual) aiming of the piece, and the servant, who eventually operated the Breda Mod. 38 machine gun, which could be installed on the top of the vehicle for anti-aircraft and short-range defence. The 75/34 Mod. S.F. cannon, designed for anti-tank fire, is always installed in the centre of the casemate on a hemispherical mount, which allows a limited swing of 20° to the right and 20° to the left, with a lift of -12° to +22°. The internal ammunition racks were also upgraded to allow the loading of 45 rounds of 75 and about 1400 bullets for the machine guns.

The increased interdiction capability of these new vehicles meant that both the Italians and the Germans used the vehicle not so much in a support or self-propelled artillery function, but mainly as a tank fighter. Like the 75/18, the new vehicle also had armour entirely bolted to an inner frame. This arrangement was not optimal, and was of outdated design; however, it facilitated the replacement of an armour element should it need to be repaired. The armour was reinforced on the sides between 25 and 30mm while the front plate was 50mm thick. On the roof, on the other hand, it retained a

▲ A 75/34 M42M self-propelled vehicle outside the Ansaldo-Fossati plant in Sestri Ponente. It was a production vehicle assembled on 26 March 1943. Source: *Gli Autoveicoli da Combattimento dell'Esercito Italiano*.

thickness of 15mm, with little armouring on the bottom or floor. Only 6mm was obviously not enough to protect against mine explosions.

The engine of the Semovente M42M was the same, but slightly upgraded, engine in use on the earlier Semovente M42 75/18 and Tank M15/42. In addition to the increase in displacement, which improved the vehicle's overall performance, the novelty was that the new engine ran on petrol instead of the diesel fuel that powered the engines of the M13/40 Tank, M14/41 Tank and the GSPs based on their hulls. The switch from diesel to petrol was due to the fact that Italian diesel reserves were almost completely exhausted by mid-1942. On the new 75/34 M42M self-propelled aircraft, thanks to the increased space in the engine compartment, the fuel tank capacity was increased to 367 litres in the main tanks, plus 40 litres in the reserve tank, making a total of 407 litres. Which in fact offered a greater operating range.

The new FIAT engine also had a revamped gearbox with five forward gears and one reverse gear, one gear more than the previous vehicles. The suspension was the same as the 75/18, of the semi-elliptical leaf spring type.

This type of suspension was obsolete and significantly slowed down the vehicle's movement. It was also very vulnerable to enemy fire or mines.

The chassis of the new M42 had 26 cm wide tracks with 86 links per side, six more than the M13/40, M14/41 and 75/18 self-propelled tanks, due to the lengthening of the hull.

The vehicle's radio supply consisted of a Radio Phonic Transceiver Equipment 1 for Tank or RF1CA Receiver Equipment. This was a radiotelephone and radiotelegraph station with a power of 10 watts for both voice and telegraphy contained in a box measuring 35 x 20 x 24.6 cm and weighing about 18 kg. It was positioned on the left side of the superstructure, behind the driver's dashboard.

The operating frequency range was between 27 and 33.4 MHz. It had a range of about 8 km in voice mode and 12 km in telegraph mode. However, these distances were drastically reduced when the self-propelled guns were in motion.

The radio antenna mounted on this new self-propelled vehicle was of a new type. Previously, the old radio antennas were more complicated to move, lower etc. and could only be done from inside the vehicle. This new, much more practical one could be lowered manually at any angle.

DATA SHEET SEMOVENTI 75/34 & 75/46		
	75/34 M42/M43	75/46
Length	5040 mm	5100 mm
Width	2230 mm	2400 mm
Height	1850 mm	1750 mm
Start and end date	1942-1945	1944-1945
Weight	15.300 kg	15.800 kg
Crew	3	3
Engine	Fiat SPA 15TB M42 petrol 8 V-cylinder, 11980 cm^3	
Maximum speed	40 km/h on road 15 km/h off road	35 km/h on road 15 km/h off road
Autonomy	200 km on road 5 h off road	180 km on road 5 h off road
Total production	145 vehicles	From 11 to 18 veicoli
Armour thickness	From 14,5 to 50 mm	From 15 to 100 mm
Armament	75/34 Mod. S.F. gun with 46 shells. Secondary: 1 Breda Mod. 38 8 mm machine gun with 1104 rounds	Ansaldo 75/46 C.A. Mod. 1934 gun with 42 shells. Secondary: 1 Breda Mod. 38 8 mm machine gun with 1000 rounds

ARMAMENT

The main weapon fitted to the 75/34 was the 75/34 Model SF [Sfera] cannon; it was derived directly from the 75/32 Model 1937 Long Range Cannon designed by the Royal Army Arsenal in Naples. As already mentioned, when the Army Staff requested a 75 mm long-barrelled cannon, Ansaldo responded with a totally new 75/36 cannon which, however, the military did not like it due to some of its deficiencies and it never went into production. The Naples Arsenal then proposed a 75/34 cannon obtained by mounting a new barrel, specially designed a few years earlier as a tank cannon. The solution from the Royal Army Arsenal in Naples was the one eventually chosen for the new self-propelled gun! It had 45 rounds available inside the casemate, together with almost 1,400 rounds of Breda ammunition.

The sight was mounted on the right side of the gun, and could be operated through a small opening hatch on the roof. It was then removed in those situations when it was not in use or when the hatch was closed. As secondary armament we always find the unfailing Breda Model 1938 8 mm Medium Machine Gun. On the 75/34 M42M Semovente the machine gun could be mounted on an anti-aircraft mount on the roof of the vehicle. When not deployed in an anti-aircraft role, the machine gun was stored on a mount on the right sponson of the combat compartment. Our self-propelled vehicle also adopted a complex system of fog grenades, introduced by copying a German system. However, this smoke curtain was only achieved at the rear of the tank, demonstrating the relative unreliability of the system.

CREW AND PRODUCTION

The crew of the vehicle consisted of three soldiers: the driver who was positioned on the left of the vehicle (to his right was the gun breech); the commander/gunner was positioned to the right of the gun breech and the loader/radio operator to the left, behind the driver. The duties assigned to the commander were to inspect the battlefield, identify targets, aim, open fire and, at the same time, give orders to the rest of the crew and listen to all messages transmitted by the radio operator. Many tasks were also assigned to the loader/serviceman, who in fact shared with the commander. In any case, the personnel on board the self-propelled vehicles were always chosen from among the best, while all the others were assigned to the medium or light tanks. These elite troops, so to speak, not only guaranteed better firing of the pieces assigned to them, but also significantly better maintenance of the self-propelled vehicle. Of all the pieces produced of the 75/34, exact numbers are not available, due to the enormous confusion that arose at the turn of the armistice, but it is estimated that there were almost 150 examples, at least those delivered up to 8 September 1943. Of all these, the Germans immediately captured 36. The Germans themselves then restarted production of the vehicle and by the end of 1943, they obtained another 50. In 1944, Ansaldo then produced a further 25 75/34 self-propelled vehicles based on the hull of the Ansaldo 105/25 M.43. This differed from its predecessors in size, being wider and lower, and in its increased armour. These vehicles, renamed StuG M43 mit 75/34 851(i), were all used only by the Germans in northern Italy and the Balkans.

CONCLUSIONS

The 75/34 M42M self-propelled gun was one of the last Italian designs to be produced before the Armistice. Overall, it had interesting features, certainly starting with the weapon being able to take on many Allied medium tanks, something its predecessors had not been able to do. On the other hand, it had many sore points and shortcomings. It was built on an inadequate chassis, cramped inside and prone to frequent breakdowns, had an insufficient crew for the required performance and was forced to perform too many tasks.

▲ Rare wartime remnant of self-propelled 75/34 preserved in Messina at the Carristi Memorial.

▲ View of the 75/34 Model SF gun mounted on trestles in the Ansaldo-Fossati factory. Source: fondazioneansaldo.com. In the small picture: the Breda Model 1938 8 mm Medium machine gun, armoured version.

▼ An out-of-service 75/34 M42M self-propelled vehicle already in German service, and captured by the Allies with other equipment.

▲ A 75/34 M42 self-propelled vehicle is loaded onto a French trailer 'La Buire'. The trailer is pulled by an M13/40 tank of the Gruppo Squadroni Armorati 'San Giusto'. The photograph was taken in the main street of Mariano del Friuli (Arena).

▲ The M42M self-propelled 75/34 in German service (see profile on opposite page) with the new folding antenna. Note also the addition of four teeth on the front sprocket.

SEMOVENTE M42 75/34 GERMAN USE

▲ Semovente M42 StuG M42 75-34 hull 851 (i) belonging to the 2nd Company 114th Panzerjager Abteilung, Rimini, Italy, summer 1944.

▲ Semovente M42 75-34 on M42 hull (StuG M42 75-34 851 (i) belonging to a German unit operating in Italy or the Balkans 1944.

SEMOVENTE 75/46

INTRODUCTION

The M43 75/46 self-propelled gun, also called the M42L (where L stood for long), being precisely 4 cm longer than the M42. It was the last self-propelled gun (SPG) produced by Italy during World War II. It was based on the earlier M43 self-propelled gun chassis, but featured a new spaced weaponry that offered better protection to the crew. It was developed by Italian companies at German request from late 1943. A total of 11 to 18 vehicles were produced, but most of the vehicles were delivered to the Germans, who deployed them on the Italian peninsula against the Allied forces in the final stages of World War II. It represented the most powerful Italian tank fighter of the Second World War.

DEVELOPMENT

The vehicle was derived from the self-propelled M43 'Bassotto', adopted by the Regio Esercito on 2 April 1943 and armed with the 105/25 howitzer, which we will discuss in the next chapter. Ansaldo's designer, engineer Giuseppe Rosini, developed the new tank destroyer by installing on the M43 hull the powerful 75/46 C.A. Mod. 1934 anti-aircraft gun, which proved to be an excellent anti-tank piece. The September armistice did not stop the programme, which was taken over by the German occupiers, with the production of 8 units in '43 and 3 in '44 renamed StuG M43 mit 75/46 852(i).

TECHNICAL FEATURES

The M43 hull used for the self-propelled was derived from that of the M.15/42 tank, enlarged and lowered, with a redesigned front and welded instead of bolted side plates. Compared to the M43 hull of the 'Dachshund', of which it retained the general mechanical and performance characteristics, that of the 75/46 self-propelled tank had reinforced armour, which was increased from 70 mm to 100 mm on the front, from 45 mm to 60 mm on the side plates and from 25 mm to 35 mm on the rear plates.

The fighting compartment consisted of the bolted and welded fixed casemate, armed with the Ansaldo 75/46 C.A. Mod. 1934 cannon on a spherical mount, with a manual swing of 34° and elevation from -12° to + 22°.

The cannon had a penetration capacity (on vertical plates) ranging from 98 mm (at a distance of 100 m) to 67 mm (at a distance of 2400 m).

The armament was completed by a Breda Mod. 38 8mm machine gun for close-range and anti-aircraft defence operated by the tank leader/cannoneer, while the radio servant/operator had a Magneti Marelli RF1 CA radio at his disposal for battery communications. The 74/46

▲ Lovely picture of the M43 75/46 self-propelled vehicle placed outside the Ansaldo-Fossati factory. In this image, the 1944 Continental camouflage and the new Breda mount are clearly visible. Author's colouring.

gun was a really good artillery gun. It had a high initial muzzle velocity due to the use of a powerful propellant and the length of the barrel, a sustained rate of fire. The gun's breech had a system for switching from manual to semi-automatic opening, with a maximum rate of fire of 15 rounds per minute with a trained crew. Its initial velocity was 800 m/s and maximum range was 8,500 m in the anti-aircraft role (the role for which the piece was designed) and 13,000 m against land targets.

■ GERMAN MODIFICATIONS

In fact, this modern self-propelled vehicle largely benefited from German engineering know-how, as the Abteilung Waffen und Gerät beim Wehrkreiskommando 6 (Weapons and Equipment Department of Military District Headquarters No. 6 in Italy) took over the industrial reins of the Italian workshops, adopting construction criteria and/or variants that brought these vehicles up to the standards useful to the German army for which they were intended.

It was they who enormously upgraded the armour, increasing the total weight by more than 600 kg. The same mounted gun was also adapted to be able to fire German Pak 40 type ammunition. In addition to the new armour plates, other upgrades were made on the Italian self-propelled vehicles produced for the Germans.

These included 4 larger teeth bolted to the outside of the gear wheel, intended to improve the efficiency of the gear wheel and its durability. Another modification requested by the Germans was to replace the right roof hatch with one that could be opened in two parts for better ventilation of the fighting compartment.

A total of six 20-litre petrol canister racks were positioned on the sides of the vehicle, three on each armoured plate spaced on the sides, just like on other Italian self-propelled guns and tanks.

It should be noted, however, that in post-1943 European, and thus German, use, on the 75/46 M43 self-propelled vehicles, petrol cans were no longer carried because they were no longer sent to North Africa, and there was no need to transport large quantities of fuel during operations in Italy or the Balkans, where the vehicle was risked. The interior of the casemate, radio equipment, engine and transmission, suspension etc. were essentially the same as the 75/34 M42M.

Final considerations on the cannon: the Germans and Ansaldo eventually decided to mount the 75/46 cannon on the M42T self-propelled vehicle, as repeatedly stated for its better anti-tank performance compared to the other Italian cannons at their disposal. However, this

▲ The gun mounted on the 75/46 was derived from the anti-aircraft piece of the same name, in the picture used by a German Flak company. Bundesarchiv. Author colouring.

choice resulted in a very low production cadence due to technical problems, especially when compared to the cadence of all other self-propelled vehicles mounted on the same chassis. Consideration was therefore given to fitting the German Panzerabwehrkanone 40 as an alternative to the 75/46. The weight of the vehicle would not have increased much, only about 70 kg. Even before the armistice, Italy and Germany made arrangements to produce the famous PaK 40 (Italian nomenclature 75/43 Cannon Model 1940) locally. By 8 September, nothing had been done except to organise a few production lines. However, for reasons unknown, the Germans, once masters of the Italian industrial fabric, did not continue this project. However, after the armistice, OTO, thanks to the production lines mentioned above, produced some spare parts for the PaK 40 for the Germans until the end of the war. The secondary armament was always the Breda Model 1938 medium machine gun with an upper magazine without anti-aircraft sights. When not in use, it was stored in the left sponson of the self-propelled gun. The machine gun was mounted on a new anti-aircraft mount attached to a crowbar that provided greater horizontal translation of the machine gun in the event of an air attack. After the Italian occupation by the Wermacht, all Bredas in gold possession were adapted for the 7.92 Mauser cartridges. As also stated in the file, the 75/46, like the previous self-propelled gun, was manned by a three-man crew. According to some unconfirmed sources it appears that the Germans preferred to add a fourth crew member behind the gunner, who would load the weapon. Obviously, adding a fourth crew member also meant drastically reducing the space inside the cramped combat compartment, which was already small for three crew members.

◼ MINISKIRTS (OSTKETTEN)

An absolute novelty on this self-propelled vehicle was the fitting of so-called Ostketten, i.e. a kind of mini-skirt that, among other things, also had a protective function for the upper part of the tracks on both sides of the vehicle. These were probably additions decided by the Germans. Like the 105/35 M43 self-propelled vehicle, the 75/46 M43 was also equipped with a side miniskirt. These were only 4 mm thick and partially protected the sides of the vehicle. Their role was not so much to protect the self-propelled vehicle from anti-tank gun bullets or shaped charge ammunition, but to prevent shrapnel from damaging the suspension and track links. The side skirts had a cut-out at the rear to allow the crew to reach the track tension regulator without having to dismantle the miniskirt.

Another three small holes were also drilled to add lubricant to the return rollers, again with the aim of not having to remove the side skirt.

▲ An M43 self-propelled 75/46 used for the training of German Panzerjäger divisions in Italy. Visible are the Nebelkerzenabwurfvorrichtung mit Schutzmantel for the use of smoke grenades.

▲ British infantry engaged in combat during the Italian campaign, operating their mortars in the presence of a bulky carcass of a 75/46 self-propelled vehicle put out of action. Interesting view of the apertures and the bottole. To the side: the radio system mounted on board the self-propelled vehicles (from the original logbook).

▼ Semovente M43 75/46 (left) next to a self-propelled M43 from 105/25 without the side skirts (right). Apart from the added main armament and armour plates, the vehicles were identical.

SEMOVENTE M42 75/46

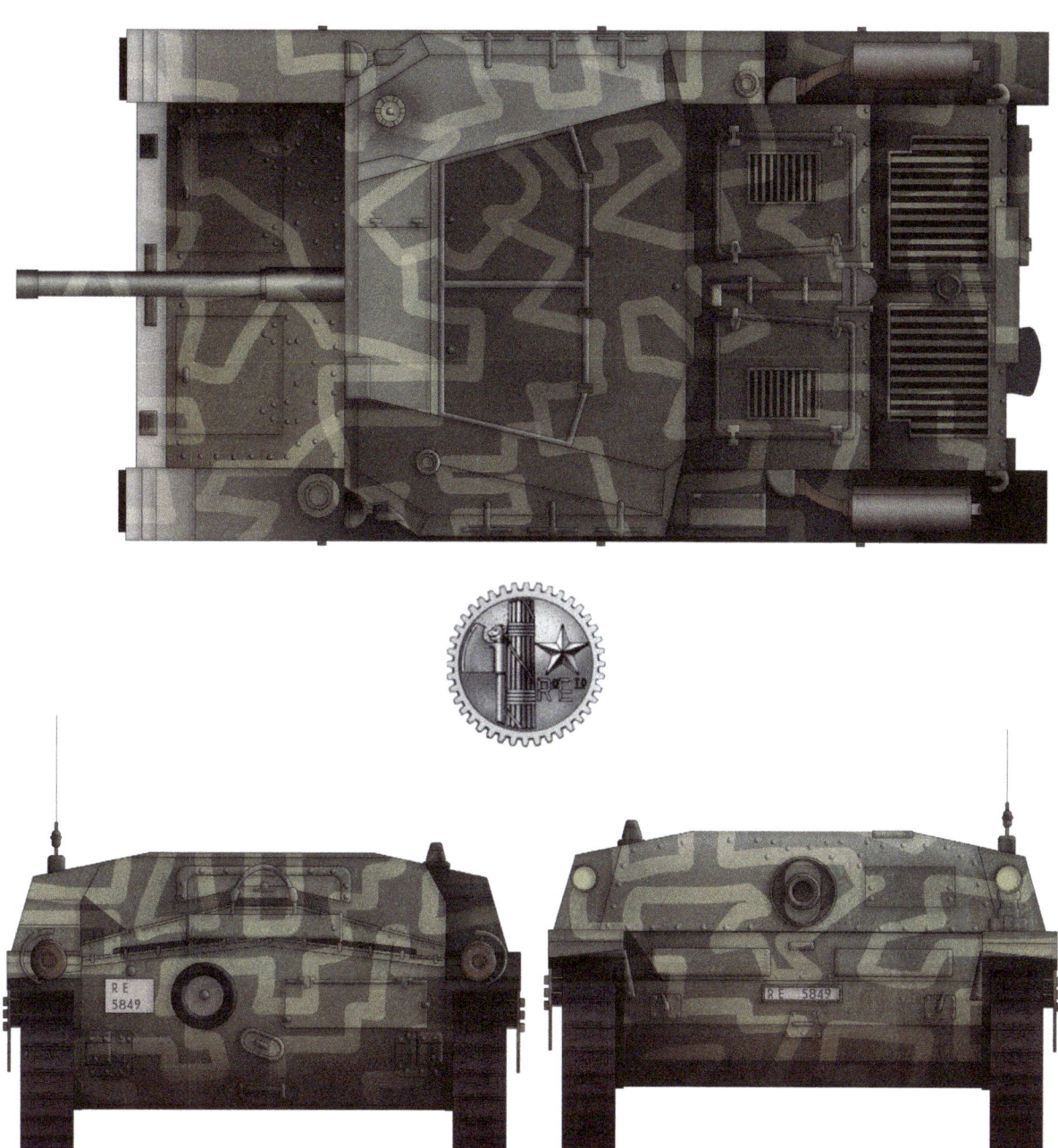

▲ View of the Italian 75/46 M43 self-propelled vehicle from above, front and rear. In the middle, the bronze or aluminium badge was placed on the top left of the front plate of the armoured vehicles from April 1936 to August 1943.

▲ Fourteen 105/25 M43s, four M15/42s and a dozen 75/34 M42Ms in the Ansaldo-Fossati factory in Genoa, ready for delivery to the Regio Esercito in July 1943. Small photo: 75/46 M43 self-propelled gun sight.

▲ The M43 self-propelled 75/46 captured in a workshop in Milan by Italian partisans at the end of April 1945.

SEMOVENTE M42T 75/46

▲ Semovente M42T 75-46 Tank destroyer version with 90° folded aerial, Italy 1943.

▲ Semovente M42 T 75-46 Version showing the special new Breda mount on the roof of the vehicle and the reserve petrol cans. Italy 1943.

SEMOVENTE M43 105-25 "DACHSUND"

▲ Semovente M43 105/25 R.E. Italy, 1943.

▲ Semovente M43 105/25 belonging to an RE unit in Italy, 1943.

SEMOVENTE 105-25

INTRODUCTION

The Ansaldo 105/25 M.43, also known as the 105/25 self-propelled gun and commonly nicknamed the Dachshund, was a valid Italian self-propelled gun used during World War II and designed by Fiat-Ansaldo, considered to be one of the most powerful self-propelled guns built by Italy in World War II. Also based on the design of the M42 75/18, it was little used by the forces of the Royal Army before the armistice, so that after the armistice signed at Cassibile and the occupation of central and northern Italy by the Germans, the self-propelled vehicles were captured and used by the German Army and the new Army of the RSI.

DEVELOPMENT

What has already been said for the self-propelled 75/34 and 46 also applies to the 105/25, which was created and put into production to overcome the objective shortcomings pointed out for the albeit good 75/18.

So, again, the development of a high-powered self-propelled vehicle was carried out during 1942 with a tender between Odero-Terni-Orlando (OTO) and FIAT-Ansaldo. The one proposed by Ansaldo was chosen because it was, among other things, more feasible and lighter, which meant it could be equipped with a less powerful petrol engine. This was a great advantage for the Italian Army, which had to replace diesel engines with petrol engines after 1942 due to limited resources. Testing of the prototype lasted several weeks. In the end, the Regio Esercito was very impressed by the firepower of the 105 mm cannon. Approved, an order followed for 130 vehicles divided into two batches, the first batch of 30 and a second of 100 self-propelled cannons. It was also officially renamed the 'Semovente FIAT-Ansaldo su scafo M43 da 105/25', abbreviated to 'Semovente M43 da 105/25', but among its crews it became known by the nickname 'Dachshund' due to its lower and wider profile. Several others were added to the first order until there were around 800 in total. The events of September '43 nipped this ambition in the bud. However, in May of the same year, twelve examples were built and used in 1943 by the 135th Armoured Division 'Aries II'.

Following the Italian surrender, the Germans, who considered the self-propelled 105/25s to be excellent vehicles, captured them and reopened the construction lines, producing a further 91 examples, renamed StuG M43 mit 105/25 853(i) and using them against Anglo-American forces. At the turn of 1944-45, one example was

▲ Interesting comparative view of a 75/18 M42 (left) and the 105/25 M43 prototype (right) at the Ansaldo-Fossati factory in Genoa. The wider and lower hull of the 'Dachshund' is evident.

also used by the RSI's 'Leoncello' Armoured Group near Brescia. The 105/25 gun was also posted in casemates in the defensive works of the Vallo Alpino.

■ TECHNICAL FEATURES

The Dachshund, following the general layout of its M42 predecessor, consisted of an M43 hull, i.e. the hull of an enlarged and lowered M15/42 tank, with a redesigned front and welded instead of bolted side plates. On the hull was a fixed casemate bolted and welded with an Ansaldo 105/25 howitzer, with a manual swing of 34° and elevation from -12° to + 22°.

The armament was complemented by a Breda Mod. 38 8 mm machine gun for close-range and anti-aircraft defence operated by the tank leader/cannoneer, while the radio servant/operator had a Magneti Marelli RF1 CA radio at his disposal for battery communications.

The hull of the M42 was 14 cm longer than its predecessors. The new hull of the M43 (also called the M42 'Long') was even longer, 4 cm longer than the M42, reaching a length of 5.10 m, 17 cm wider and 10 cm lower. All these modifications added up to a total vehicle weight of 15.8 combat-ready tonnes compared to the M42's 15 tonnes.

This made the silhouette of the vehicle more elusive and low and also allowed the gun to be positioned in the centre of the superstructure, instead of being moved to the right, as on the previous chassis of the 75/18.

The armour was both bolted to an inner frame and welded (a necessary improvement for Italian vehicles) and was finally thicker than Italian standards. The hull armour was 50 mm at the top and 25 mm at the bottom. The superstructure had 70 mm thick armour at the front, 45 mm at the sides, while at the rear it was protected by a 35 mm thick plate.

A plate of the same thickness protected the rear part of the engine compartment. The roof and floor of the vehicle were 15 mm thick.

New for the vehicle were the so-called Ostketten, i.e. side skirts divided into three parts.

These were 4/5 mm thick. They partially protected the sides of the vehicle. The side skirts had a hole in the rear to allow the crew to reach the track tension regulator. The good armour reinforcement was partly rendered futile by the fact that the Italian industry was unable to supply good quality ballistic steel. As a result, although thick, Italian armour was fragile compared to armour of equal thickness from other nations involved in the war.

▲ Some officers of the DC Gruppo Semoventi pose in front of a brand new 105/25 M43 self-propelled vehicle that had just been delivered to the unit at the Nettunia range in the late summer of 1943 (Pignato).

When an enemy shell struck the Italian armour, it would often break or splinter even without being pierced, causing damage to the vehicle and often to the crew members, very often forcing the units to send the vehicle to specialist workshops to replace the damaged armour plates. The external bodywork had some new features. The most obvious was the longer and wider casemate than that of the 75/18. On the roof, on the left side, was the radio antenna, which could now be folded down in a more practical manner, a fully rotatable periscope and an opening for the cannon. The commander was equipped with an optical sighting system manufactured by Ansaldo and weighing around 13 kg. On the rear and sides of the vehicle were a jack stand, storage compartments and other tools. On the sides of the casemate were two headlights for night operations. The engine compartment was equipped with grilles for cooling the engine.

Behind them were the fuel tank cap and two radiator cooling grids. At the rear were a spare wheel, a hole for the engine crank, the tow hook and a complex smoke grenade launcher system consisting of a grenade launcher and a smoke grenade rack for reloading the grenade launcher.

Unfortunately, this only worked at the rear of the vehicle and also bored the sides or the front of the vehicle.

On the sides of the rear area were mufflers covered by a steel shield to protect them from impact. On the sides of the vehicle were six racks, three per side, for 20-litre petrol cans, just like on other Italian self-propelled and armoured vehicles. This equipment was particularly designed for the African theatre where the canisters would increase the vehicle's autonomy.

It should be noted, however, that in most cases, on the M43 self-propelled 105/25 tanks were not transported because, in Italy, it was not that difficult to find fuel. For the suspension, we refer to the previous chapter on the self-propelled 75/46.

▲ A self-propelled 105/25 loaded onto a fast transport trailer to be transported to the operational area. State Archives. Author's colouring. Small photo: an M43 self-propelled 105/25 captured by the Germans in Rome after the Armistice. Note the original Regio Esercito plate, RE 6453. Rome, March 1944.

▲ A StuG M43 105/25 captured by the Germans. Photo taken a few days after the Armistice. Author's colouring.
▼ Souvenir photo of German soldiers standing on the roof of a self-propelled 105/25. Author's colouring.

SEMOVENTE M43 105-25 "DACHSUND"

▲ Semovente M43 105/25 mounted on M15/42 chassis belonging to the RSI's Leoncello armoured division, Italy February 1945.

▲ Semovente M42L/43 105-25 on M42L hull (StuG M 43 105-25 853 (i) of the 2nd Battery 914th Sturmgeschutz Brigade, Italy, summer 1944.

ARMAMENT

The main variation in all Italian self-propelled vehicles lies in the cannon. In this case, the main armament was a 105/25 howitzer (sometimes also called the Mod. SF 'Sferico') produced by Ansaldo. It was developed on the basis of the 105/23 Mod. 1942 howitzer, which in turn was developed from an OTO-Melara howitzer as a prototype for divisional artillery together with the 105/40 Mod. 1938 howitzer. Unfortunately for the Italian Armed Forces, the new gun was tested and thus produced too late, thus having little effect on the state of the conflict. At least two prototypes of the 105/23 Mod. 1942 howitzer were produced.

One, or perhaps more, were on field mounts and one on a spherical mount intended for the prototype of the M43 105/25 self-propelled gun. The field version of the gun intended for the dachshund had a maximum range of 13 km and a range of 2,000-2,500 m with anti-tank ammunition. It had a practical rate of fire of 8 rounds per minute. Obviously, within the narrow combat compartment of the self-propelled gun, this cadence decreased dramatically.

The weight of the weapon is not stated in the sources, it can be estimated at something less than a tonne together with its spherical mount. As a reference, the 105/28 Mod. 1912 cannon, also produced by Ansaldo and of similar type and ammunition, had a barrel length of 2.987 m (compared to 2.6 m for the 105/25) and weighed 850 kg. Due to the extension of the vehicle, the spherical cannon mount was placed centrally on the front plate. The cannon had a horizontal translation of 18° to the right and 18° to the left, as well as an elevation of +18° and a depression of -10°. As always, the secondary armament consisted of a Breda Mod. 38, the vehicle version of the Breda Mod. 37 medium machine gun used by the Italian infantry. The machine gun weighed 15.4 kg and was prepared for the Breda 8×59 RB cartridge. The Breda Mod. 38 had a theoretical rate of fire of 600 rounds per minute, which in practice dropped to around 350 rounds per minute.

One of the advantages of this machine gun, besides its reliability, was its small size. In fact, the machine gun was only 89 cm long and took up little space when stored inside the vehicle.

In addition to the Breda, the crew also had the official Carcano Mod. 91, or MAB 38 machine guns and 35 hand grenades for close defence against enemy infantry. The engine, crew, radio system and division of the interior space of the self-propelled vehicle are similar to those already described in the other self-propelled vehicles in this volume.

▲ A photo of the 105/25 M43 self-propelled vehicle of the 'Leoncello' Group. The vehicle bears the battle name 'TERREMOTO' on the front of the casemate and also appears to have a number plate. On board the vehicle is Captain Zuccaro. Several copies of this photograph were distributed to the Group's Carristi and on the back bore a dedication by the commander similar to this one: 'For Domenico Noè in the certainty of his loyalty to the end! Captain Zuccaro P.d.C. 867 13.3 XXIII' (Arena archive).

▲ A 105/25 rendered unserviceable and then abandoned by its German crew is inspected by a British soldier. Clearly visible through the open hatch is the FIAT-SPA T15B engine.

DATA SHEET SEMOVENTE 105/25 M43	
Length	5100 mm
Width	2400 mm
Height	1750 mm
Start and end date	1943-1945
Weight	15.800 kg
Crew	3
Engine	Fiat SPA 15TB M42 petrol 8 V-cylinder, 11980 cm^3
Maximum speed	35 km/h on road and 15 km/h off road
Autonomy	180 km on-road or 5 h off-road
Total production	121 vehicles
Armour thickness	From 15 mm, to 45 mm lateral to 70 mm frontal
Armament	Ansaldo 105/25 howitzer with 48 shells. Secondary: 1 Breda Mod. 38 8 mm machine gun with 864 rounds

SEMOVENTE M41M 90/53

▲ Semovente M41M 90/53 self-propelled gun. Proving ground in Nettunia (Roma) late 1942 Italy

▲ Semovente M41M 90/53 of the CLXIII Gruppo Controcarri Semoventi in Sicily sand-yellow camouflage version, Sicily, Italy, July 1943.

SEMOVENTE 90/53

INTRODUCTION

The 90/53 self-propelled gun was an armoured artillery gun also used as a tank destroyer, produced in Italy during the Second World War based on the idea of Colonel Sergio Berlese, an esteemed Italian designer and member of the Artillery Technical Service. The armament consisted of a 53-calibre (L/53) Mod. 1939 90/53 cannon. Between 30 and 48 examples were produced during 1942.

DEVELOPMENT

In the course of Operation Barbarossa, the powerful and innovative Soviet T-34 and KV-1 tanks appeared, equipped with armour and armament superior to the standards of the time. These proved to be a tough opponent even for the best-equipped German tanks, let alone the Italian armed forces.

The Italian Expeditionary Corps in Russia (CSIR), which arrived on the Eastern Front in July 1941, saw this huge disadvantage at first hand.

Initially, the idea was therefore to use a firearm originally designed for anti-aircraft firing in a kind of new anti-tank function.

Somewhat emulating the success achieved by the Germans with their 88 mm Flak. The Italian General Staff therefore opted for the 90/53 90 mm anti-aircraft gun produced by Ansaldo. It had similar, and in some areas even better, performance than the 88-mm Flak series. The design was based from the beginning on the M13/40 tank hull, then time was lost waiting to decide which gun tube to adopt.

Finally, in December 1941, the plans for the new Ansaldo 90/53 Mod 39 cannon were ready. The complete design was finalised in January 1942, and the first prototypes were set up and the first tests carried out. On 5 March of the same year, a working model was taken to firing tests at the special bench at the Ansaldo-Fossati factory in Sestri Ponente.

Five months after these trials, the first six actual examples were already assembled.

▲ Members of the Italian crew (the first on the left is Dino Landini) posing for souvenir photos probably after the 90/53 training in Nettuno, near Rome.

■ TECHNICAL FEATURES

The cannon was mounted on the hull of the M14/41, which was lengthened by 17 cm to better fit the weapon system and with the rear suspension shifted backwards; this was very important as it allowed the cannon to be placed in a considerably rearward position. This shrewdness made it possible, among other things, to greatly facilitate firing operations.

This resulted in an ideal solution, with the only major drawback of not being able to obtain a casemate or adequate space for the crew of the vehicle.

So the servants had to travel in a separate vehicle. The crew actually on board the self-propelled vehicle therefore consisted only of the pilot and the tank leader. The gun carriage underwent several modifications to be adapted to the M14's hull: the cradle was redesigned in order to move the trunnions to a barycentric position, the balancers, the underbelly and related manoeuvring parts, and the shielding were removed.

The range covered an arc of 40° to the right and 40° to the left, while the elevation ranged from -5° to +24°. The piece proved to be an effective anti-tank weapon, capable of piercing even heavy Mk VIII Churchills with front armour more than 100 mm thick, provided the targets were less than 500 metres away.

The main shortcoming of the vehicle was the lack of space in general, and not only for the crew, but also for ammunition: each self-propelled vehicle could therefore only carry eight grenades, the difference being that eighty-six were transported on an L6/40 light tank suitably modified as an ammunition carrier, which could also serve as a transport for the other two crew members. As a self-propelled artillery vehicle operating at a good distance from the front line, the vehicle maintained a modest armour plating: the hull was 30 mm thick at the front, 25 mm on the sides and rear, 15 mm for the roof and 6 mm on the bottom; the small superstructure also acting as a cape was 41 mm thick and sloping at 28° (sloping compared to vertical armour). Finally, the cannon shield was 30mm thick.

Behind the shield are the two gunners with their seat positions aligned. The main defect of the 90/53 was due to the fact that it was designed for anti-aircraft fire only (unlike the German 88mm), and therefore lacked spe-

▲ Close-up of an M41M 90/53 self-propelled vehicle with the Regio Esercito 5824 licence plate.

SEMOVENTE M41M 90/53

▲ Semovente M41M 90/53 Beute Gepanzerte-Selbstfahrlafette of the 26th Panzer Division, Italy 1943-45.

▲ Semovente M41 90-53 (R.E. 5825) of the 163rd Artillery Support Group, Sicily, July 1943

ITALIAN SEMOVENTI WWII

cific ammunition dedicated to anti-tank fire, and therefore operated with a generic armour-piercing projectile, which did not do justice to the (excellent) quality of the gun. It also lacked an EP (ready effect) projectile, i.e. the Italian equivalent of the hollow charge. Thus, although very powerful for the average Italian, the 90/53 was for many reasons a big missed opportunity. It missed its goal of becoming an outstanding weapon due to the above-mentioned shortcomings. Another serious shortcoming of the 90/53 self-propelled gun was the fact that long and laborious operations were required before opening fire; therefore, its use could only be envisaged in a static environment and not in mobile warfare conditions. For this reason, seeing these limitations, it was decided not to send it either to Africa or Russia where it would not be able to operate at its best. The light armouring and the open structure of the gun also did not protect the artillerymen from enemy infantry fire and even worse from attack by low-flying machine-gun aircraft. Finally, the need to share ammunition on one vehicle, typically the L6/40 tank transport version, and the gun exposed the entire gun-and-crew system to great reliability risks, which were well understood by the Italian armoured unit commanders once their superiors had already started to produce this self-propelled unit. In practice, for all these reasons, it was not recommended for use as an anti-tank gun (which was what they were trying to achieve), and consequently, doubts were also raised as a self-propelled support gun (the 90 mm was 'only' a direct-firing piece, not an indirect-firing piece like the 75/18, or direct-indirect like the 75/34 and 105/28, used by the other Italian self-propelled units). For this reason, despite the great need for modern tanks on all fronts, the use of this self-propelled unit was postponed and all but forgotten, being used only and with little success in Sicily during the Allied landings.

CONCLUSIONS

Many sources and several armoured vehicle enthusiasts consider the 90/53 M41M self-propelled gun to be a poorly designed self-propelled gun that, apart from the powerful main gun, had nothing exceptional about it. In addition to the shortcomings we have already pointed out, it must also be said that all the crews came from artillery regiments and had basic training in static artillery equipment or at best truck repair. They received only limited and too quick training on armoured vehicle repair at the Nettuno training school before being transferred to Sicily. Of the two theatres for which the vehicle was designed, the Russian one would not have been ideal, while perhaps the African front would have offered more opportunities for this type of weapon. Basically, it remains that made as a tank fighter, in fact it never did, due to what has been said and also due to the very small number of vehicles produced.

▲ Semovente da 90/53 of the CLXIII Group abandoned by the Italians near Canicattì. Source: Sicily 1943.

SEMOVENTE M41M 90/53

▲ Semovente M41M 90/53 Unidentified unit, Regio Escercito - Southern Italy, 1943.

▲ Hypothetical study for the realisation of the 149/40 self-propelled vehicle on an M41 hull that was never built. Italy 1943.

▲ Front side view of the M41M 90/53 in force at the Regio Esercito in camouflage colours.
▼ Rear view of the M41M 90/53, in which the shielded castle of the 90 gun can be clearly seen.

▲ M41M 90/53 self-propelled aircraft at Ansaldo-Fossati. The white roundel on the roof of the superstructure was painted for aerial recognition. Source: Ansaldo.

▼ The ammunition transport vehicle, made from the L6/40 converted from the Ansaldo-Fossati plant, towing a Viberti supplementary ammunition trailer. Source: Ansaldo.

SEMOVENTE M42 149/40

▲ Semovente 149/40 M42 original prototype camouflage version, Royal Army, Italy 1943.

▲ Semovente 149/40 M42 original prototype Regio Esercito, Italy 1943.

SEMOVENTE 149/40

INTRODUCTION

The 149/40 self-propelled vehicle was an Italian prototype self-propelled vehicle powered by a 183.44 kW (246 hp) SPA engine and armed with a 149 mm artillery piece. It was a gun installation, the largest ever conceived for an Italian self-propelled vehicle!

DEVELOPMENT

Ansaldo, which produced the 149/40 mm Mod. 1935 field gun with mechanical drive, thought that a self-propelled version on a tracked hull might be a good idea and would be less expensive and more practical to use. In 1942, the management of the Artillery Works decided to proceed with the construction of a prototype to be submitted to the Royal Army.

The hull was built from scratch, on which the 149 mm piece would be mounted at the rear, combined with the steering assembly type taken from the M15/42, with suspension taken from the P26/40 model suitably strengthened to withstand the weight of the gun. And finally to a powerful engine, the 246 hp SPA 228 petrol engine.

The design was started in April 1942 and the prototype was ready in August 1943, the same month it carried out some firing trials in Genoa. It was planned to produce 20 units by December 1943, but the peculiar political moment caused production to be abandoned. So only the prototype remained. A few days after the firing trials, the prototype was requisitioned by the Germans, who re-designated it gepanzerte Selbstfahrlette M 43 mit 15 cm L/42 854(i). The 149/40 self-propelled gun was transferred by rail to Hillersleben in Germany, where it was later found by US troops and transferred to the United States of America to the Aberdeen Proving Ground in Harford County in the state of Maryland.

ARMAMENT

The armament coincides with the Ansaldo 149/40 Mod. 1935 howitzer alone. It had a maximum range of almost

▲ The only example of the self-propelled 149/40 is now housed in an open-air museum in the United States, at the US Army Ordnance Museum in Aberdeen.

22 km, with an initial speed of 800 m/s and a firing cadence of about one shot per minute as normal (equal to 60 shots per hour).

Battery firing was only possible with ground ploughshares, which, however, made an excellent impression both in terms of stability and the ability to operate on all types of terrain. In addition, compared to the 149/40 self-propelled piece, it had the advantage that it could be quickly put into position, required less manpower, was protected in its propulsion organs and weighed less (24 tonnes as opposed to 32 for the gun and two tractors for transport).

■ CREW

Like most information concerning this obscure vehicle, the number of men required to operate it effectively is unknown. Sources often mention that the vehicle had only two crew members, but this probably refers, as in the case of the relative 90/53, only to those who were stationed inside the vehicle. This would include the driver and probably the commander, but could also be any member of the crew. The rest of the crew would again presumably be transported in an auxiliary vehicle. Ideally, to keep up with the 149/40 M43 self-propelled vehicle, a fully tracked vehicle would be used in this role.

■ CONCLUSION

The M43 self-propelled 149/40 was certainly a rather interesting Italian vehicle with a modern concept for the times. It was designed and built with the intention of providing mobility for heavier weapons. Unfortunately, the notoriously serious Italian industrial situation, the lack of resources and the concomitant need for armoured vehicles of all types caused this project to be shelved.

▲ Interesting photo of the 149/40 M43 self-propelled prototype, captured by the Allies in Germany, and then taken to this military depot near Paris in 1944, before ending up in the USA. Author's colouring.

SEMOVENTE M42 149/40

▲ Semovente 149/40 M42 German service camouflage version, 1943-1945.

DATA SHEET SEMOVENTI 90/53 & 149/40		
	M41 90/53	**M43 149/40**
Length	5210 mm	6500 mm
Width	2200 mm	3000 mm
Height	2150 mm	2000 mm
Start and end date	1942-1945	1943
Weight	17.000 kg	24.000 kg
Crew	4	3
Engine	Fiat SPA 15TM 41 petrol 8-cylinder VV engine (90/53) SPA 250 VV petrol engine (149/490)	
Maximum speed	25 km/h on road	35 km/h on road
Autonomy	200 km on road	180 km on road
Total production	From 30 to 50	One prototype
Armour thickness	From 15 to 30 mm	From 15 to 25 mm
Armament	90/53 gun Mod. 1939	Ansaldo gun 149/40 Mod. 1935

ITALIAN SEMOVENTI WWII

▲ The only example of the self-propelled 149/40 is now housed in an open-air museum in the United States, at the US Army Ordnance Museum in Aberdeen.

◄ Beautiful view of the breech of the self-propelled aircraft preserved in the USA. Well maintained, it has received several non-original paint jobs over the years.

▼ The elevation of the self-propelled M43 149/40 gun was the same as the towed version, but the translation was slightly lower at 53°. Source: Ansaldo Archives. Author's colouring.

OPERATIONAL USE

■ **OPERATIONAL CAMPAIGNS** (*of all self-propelled vehicles*)

Due to the dramatic period the Italian armed forces went through during 1943, the Royal Army received a very small number of self-propelled 75/34 of the 280 planned. Of the divisions that were destined to receive them, at least one self-propelled unit was reported for the Cavalry Regiment 'Cavalleggeri di Alessandria'. The Ariete Armoured Cavalry Division, formed on 1 April 1943, and its CXXXV Battalion Semoventi Controcarri, received fewer than 20 self-propelled vehicles. With these few forces, the Division, now renamed 135th D.C Ariete II, was ordered in September to contribute to the defence of Rome by Marshal Badoglio, with its armoured battalion stationed in the area of the Roman Castles at Cesano. However, the unit, placed north of Rome, ended up surrendering to the former Allies on 10 September.

The 75/46, on the other hand, had an operational life that is little known today, as it operated mainly with German forces. It is known that it was part of plans for units made up of German Panzerjäger squadrons and German-equipped Italian tank fighters. Then it was certainly used by some Germanic formations whose possible equipment has only been speculated upon, such as the 26th panzer division, or the 148th infantry division as part of its armoured units.

The 105/25 'Dachshund' was also produced in low numbers before September 43. Of these, 12 were used in 1943 by the 135th Armoured Division 'Ariete II', which clashed with German troops near Rome in the days following the Italian government's Armistice, on 8 and 9 September 1943, and gave an excellent performance. These are the main facts. Immediately after the Armistice, the German command, which had long foreseen the Italian defection, launched Fall Achse (Operation Axis), intended to dismantle the entire Royal Italian Army.

On 9 September 1943, the morning after the radio announcement of the Armistice, the 135th Armoured Division engaged German troops in the town of Cesano and on the Via Ostiense leading to Rome. It is still very difficult to establish in which part of Rome these units took part in the fighting, as the Armoured Division fought in many quarters of Rome, such as in support of the 21st Infantry Division 'Granatieri di Sardegna' at Porta San Paolo, or with members of the Italian Africa Police and the 18th Bersaglieri Regiment near the Colosseum.

During all the fighting, four M43 Semoventi da 105/25 of the DCI° Gruppo Corazzato were destroyed. It is unclear whether they were all destroyed by German weapons or whether some were sabotaged by the crews before escaping and in some cases joining the Italian partisan resistance. For the record, the German operation called Fall Achse lasted until 19 September 1943 and resulted in

▲ Interesting picture showing the crew of a 90/53 self-propelled vehicle in full, intent on loading the piece. Note also the ammunition carrier carved out of the hull of the L6/40, equipped among other things with a Breda machine gun for close-range defence. Crippa Archive. Author's colouring.

the death of more than 20,000 Italian soldiers, the capture of more than one million Italian soldiers, almost 3,500 anti-tank or anti-aircraft guns, howitzers or field guns, 16,600 trucks or cars and about a thousand armoured or armoured vehicles. A real debacle that gives an idea of the great confusion and disorganisation of the Italian army and especially its leadership in those days. Among the numerous captured armoured vehicles were the 26 surviving M43 Semoventi M43 mit 105/25, which were later renamed Beutepanzer Sturmgeschütz M43 mit 105/25 853(i). For the duration of the war, the Germans had another 91 StuG M43 mit 105/25 853(i) produced after the armistice. This meant that the Wehrmacht used a total of 116 M43 mit 105/25. The Germans themselves, who considered the self-propelled 105/25s to be excellent vehicles, employed them effectively against the Anglo-American forces. The 90/53 self-propelled gun was planned to serve on the Eastern Front. And the planned groups using the thirty available were organised in the spring of 1942. Departure for Russia was planned for October of the same year.

However, at the last moment, the destination changed and the vehicles had to reach Sicily for the defence of the island. Here the vehicles arrived in December of the same year. They had their baptism of fire during the Allied landings in July 1943. On the Licata front, they lost three self-propelled vehicles in the fighting.

On 17 July, only a few self-propelled vehicles remained useful. In the end, none of the armoured vehicles were able to be transported to the continent and thus all the equipment was lost in battle or captured. This was also the last time these vehicles went into battle with Italian forces. After the armistice, some pieces left in Nettuno were instead used by the Germans. They christened the vehicles Beute Gepanzerte-Selbstfahrlafette 9.0 cm KwK L/53 801(i) and assigned them to the Stabskompanie of the Panzer-Regiment of the 26ª Panzer Division. Only one vehicle was deployed by the unit in the Chieti area.

■ SERVING THE RSI

After the armistice, Benito Mussolini was freed by the Germans from his imprisonment on the Gran Sasso. Under German pressure, a new state was then immediately created in the Italian territories not yet under Allied control, the German-allied Italian Social Republic. This was essentially a puppet state under German control. Some of the new vehicles lost from the control of the royal army competed in the republican army, few in truth since the Germans took them all for themselves. A 75/34 was assigned to the 'San Giusto' Armoured Squadron Group. However, it remained in repair for the remainder of the conflict. The other armoured unit, the Leonessa framed in the GNR, was assigned 24 75/34 self-propelled vehicles on paper. In reality, it seems that none of these vehicles ever reached the unit, which was assigned to some German Panzerjäger-Abteilung operating in Italy. At the turn of 1944-45, a 105/25 Bassotto was also used by the RSI's 'Leoncello' Armoured Group near Brescia.

■ PARTISAN SEMOVENTI

In the hectic days of the end of the conflict, some vehicles passed into the hands of partisan formations. The first of these vehicles, a 75/34, was found by the partisans still in the workshop in Turin, along with two M14/42 tanks participating in a truly surrealist battle against Nazi-Fascist forces inside the workshop. A 75/46 had a similar fate, not in Turin but in Milan: the partisans took possession of a vehicle found abandoned at the workshops of the Milanese Steel Foundry Vanzetti SA.

▲ A self-propelled 105/25 (StuG M43) well camouflaged and abandoned by its servants in an area near Neptune is inspected by Allied soldiers. Author colour.

▼ The self-propelled 75/34 captured and then taken on 'parade' in Turin by the partisans. (Photo: Paolo Crippa archive).

MODELLISM & SELF-PROPELLED

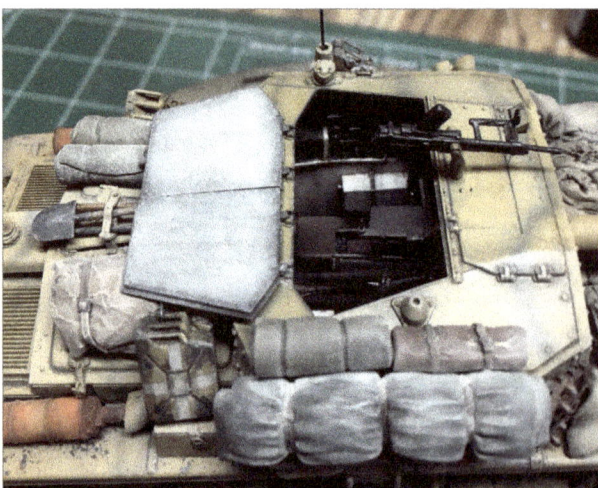

▲ Diversi particolari di modellini del semovente 75/18 M14/41 delle marche Model Victoria, e della Tamyia. Opere di fiversi autori di vari club di modellismo. Foto effettuate presso mostre di concorsi e altro.

CAMOUFLAGE AND MARKINGS

The background colours of Italian self-propelled vehicles of all types from their creation until 1945, (the operational period of such use is indicated in brackets) also used for all armoured vehicles, were:

- grey green R.E. (1936-1945)
- dark chocolate (1936-1941)
- reddish brown (1936-1943)
- ochre (for prototypes)
- sand (1941-1945)
- dark sand (1943-1945)
- dark grey (1941-1943).

Camouflage was used:
- medium green (1936-1943)
- dark red (for prototypes).

Self-propelled vehicles were not yet born at the time of the Ethiopian War 1935-1936 and the Spanish Civil War 1937-1939.

National territory 1936-1940 - substantial prevalence of grey-green.

Occupation of Albania and the French Front 1939-1940 - grey green.

Campaign in Greece and Yugoslavia 1940-1941 - grey-green possibly camouflaged with green and sand-coloured specks.

East Africa 1940-1941 - grey green or in the old Ethiopian campaign camouflage reddish brown with green spots.

North Africa 1940-1943 - at first only grey-green, the colour in which they were generally disembarked at destination ports, then sand colour in various variegated versions. Not used in the Russian Campaign 1941-1943.

RSI 1943-1945 green-grey, dark sand yellow, reddish brown with medium dense green speckling, in German panzer grey uniform colour. In particular, the 'Leonessa' and 'San Giusto' tanks were dark sand-coloured. I also note the presence of elaborate camouflage in irregular chequered patterns with a sandy yellow background and green and brown patches.

BADGES

In order to recognise individual armoured vehicles in military operations, even for Italy, it became necessary to introduce an identification system, also because at least initially there were no tanks with radio equipment installed. Radios, in fact, only began to be installed with some regularity from 1941 onwards. In the beginning, flags with red or white drapes were used for communication. The first table of distinctive tank markings dates back to 1925 and was very complex and articulated, to the point of excess. Number groups were not introduced until 1927, after the establishment of the Tank Regiment; new regulations were issued in 1928.

These official tables never mentioned the markings **for self-propelled vehicles.** It so happened that many units followed their directives, while others went their own way. Thus the most disparate symbols appeared on the hulls, from the black tortoise of the ram division to the centaur with a bow on horseback for the division of the same name. Colourful geometric figures (circles, triangles or rhombuses) of various sizes were used. Soon, however, the use of triangles (typical of self-propelled vehicles only) became standardised, at least in the 'Aries'. These were triangles with the tip pointing downwards, and inverted in the case of command tanks. They were either single-coloured or two-coloured in the colour choices already adopted for the tanks: the first battery had red, the $2^{nd(a)}$ blue, the $3^{rd(a)}$ yellow, the $4^{th\,a}$ green; white was reserved for the command tanks. The first batteries had a single-coloured triangle. The triangles of the various batteries were surmounted by an Arabic number (of the colour of the battery) indicating the self-propelled unit in the organic formation of the department.

Some of the self-propelled units adopted coloured guidons on the radio antennas, the same colour for each group: for example, the DLIV group had red cloth guidons with a different central yellow geometric design for each of the twelve self-propelled units in the division. These symbols, for this group belonging to the Littorio Division, were also painted, again in red, on the rear bulkhead of the casemate.

The self-propelled vehicles of the CCXXX Assault Group operating in Sicily in 1943, instead of the triangle, used as a badge a sort of black guidon, also triangular, with the effigy of a skull resting on white crossbones (see page 46). Each vehicle could also be distinguished by a precise name written in white on a rectangle on a red background on the side of the hull, which also served as an identification code for radio calls. The first battery of the DLVII group, for example, chose the names of the great Italian condottieri of the Renaissance: Fieramosca, Biancamano, Malatesta, Carmagnola,

Montecuccoli, Colleoni and Fortebraccio, while the self-propelled vehicles of the 2nd battery used the names of ancient weapons: Arrow, Sling, Strale, Picca, Dardo and Alabarda.

Other groups adopted the name of old rifles and artillery such as: Archibugio, Spingarda, Colubrina etc. (see pages 31 and 43).

Several self-propelled vehicles, in honour of the fact that they belonged to the artillery, bore the armoured artillery emblem (crossed cannons surmounted by a grenade and horizontal flame) painted on the front right side of the casemate (as a rule, it was on the left side). With time, however, the self-propelled tanks increasingly adopted the coloured rectangles already in use on medium and light tanks. The self-propelled batteries were represented by coloured rectangles in the manner already indicated for triangles. As a sign of aerial identification, a white Savoy cross was sometimes painted on the vehicles, placed, depending on the type of vehicle, on the turret or engine compartment ceiling.

As of 1941, a white disc of about 70 cm in diameter was painted instead of the cross. Despite circulars and instructions as already mentioned, there were numerous exceptions and variations to the official regulations.

The self-propelled vehicles that later passed into the hands of the Italian Social Republic showed the distinctive signs of the various units painted on them: the 'Leonessa' had a slightly more complicated distinguishing sign consisting of the red M of Mussolini, cut by a black bundle and underneath the inscription 'GNR', also in black. The 'San Giusto' Armoured Squadron Group adopted a symbol consisting of a simple tricolour, to which the outline of a black tank was added from the spring of 1944.

The tricolour was later (autumn 1944) replaced with a waving one and the silhouette of the tank with that of a self-propelled vehicle. The self-propelled vehicles captured and later reused by the Germans, (and besides these also the new ones ordered after the armistice of 1944) bore the typical German army markings starting with the black and white *Ritterkreuz* in its various shapes. The same was true for the camouflage, with 'German' colours for the vehicles that joined the German army.

COLORI E MIMETICHE REGIO ESERCITO WW2

 verde medio chiaro 1936-1943 mimetico
 grigio verde 1936-1945 fondo
 bruno rossiccio 1936-1943 fondo
 sabbia chiaro 1941-1945 fondo
 sabbia scuro 1943-1945 fondo
 sabbia alternativo 1941-1945 fondo
 verde scuro 1936-1943 mimetico

 gun metal-cingoli
 gomma scura cingoli
 panzer grey 1943-1945 fondo
 tuta carristi
 khaki nord Africa
 rosso minio carri
 bianco avorio interno

BIBLIOGRAPHY

- Miglia, F. *(1978). Il Carro di Rottura da 8 ton.*
- T. L. Jentz (2008) *Panzer tracts No. 19-2 Beute Panzerkampfwagen, carri armati britannici, americani, russi e italiani catturati dal 1940 al 1945*
- B. Dumitrijević, D. Savić *Oklopne jedinice na Jugoslovenskom ratištu, Institut za savremenu istoriju, Beograd*
- F. Cappellano e PP Battistelli (2012) *Carri armati leggeri italiani 1919-45*, Nuova Avanguardia
- F. Cappellano e PP Battistelli *Carri armati medi italiani 1939-45 ; New Vanguard Book 195 – Osprey Publishing*, 20 dicembre 2012
- F. Cappellano e N. Pignato – *Gli autoveicoli da combattimento dell'Esercito Italiano, Vol.1 e 2 (1940-1945).*
- F. Cappellano e N. Pignato *Andare contro i carri armati. L'evoluzione della difesa controcarro nell'esercito italiano dal 1918 al 1945 – Udine 2008*
- F. Cappellano, *Le artiglierie del Regio Esercito nella seconda guerra mondiale, Parma, AES, 1998*
- N. Pignato – *Armi della fanteria Italiana Nella Seconda Guerra Mondiale*
- N. Pignato – *Semovente da 75/18 : tecnica e storia del primo semovente italiano.* (2010).Parma: Albertelli.
- N. Pignato – *I mezzi blindo-corazzati italiani 1923-1943*, Storia Militare, 2005.
- N. Pignato - *Military vehicle prints series nr. 37.* Bellona Polonia.
- N. Pignato - *Italian Armored Vehicles of World War Two.* (2004). Squadron/Signal publications.
- N. Pignato – *Storia dei mezzi corazzati.* Vol. II. Fratelli Fabbri Editori.
- N. Pignato, (2001). *Italian Medium Tanks in action.* Squadron/Signal Publications, USA
- Rosini, G. *(1938). L'Armamento dei Carri Armati.* Reprinted (2021). FWD Publishing, USA
- Archivio FIAT
- Archivio AREP
- Daniele Guglielmi. *Semoventi M41 e M42.* Armor Photogallery -Broncos (in inglese)
- D. Guglielmi A. e D. Tallillo *Carro M – Carri Medi M11/39, M13/40, M14/41, M15/42, Semoventi ed Altri Derivati Volume Primo e Secondo - Gruppo Modellistico Trentino di Studio e Ricerca Storica, 2012*
- Falessi, Cesare; Pafi, Benedetto *Veicoli da Combattimento dell'Esercito Italiano dal 1939 al 1945.*(1976). Intyrama books.
- Janusz Ledwoch *Tank Power vol. CLXXXIII 443. Semovente da 75/32-34-46, 90/53, 105/25* -Polonia Widawnictwo militaria.
- Janusz Ledwoch *Semovente da 75/18. Tank Power vol. CXII 365* - Polonia Widawnictwo militaria.
- Janusz Ledwoch *Mussolini Tanks - Tank Powwer vol. XXIX.* Polonia Widawnictwo militaria.
- Kosar, F. *(1974). Light Fieldguns.* Ian Allen Publishing, UK
- Stern, A. *(circa 1940). Notes of presentations to Tank Board circa 1940.*
- Lorenzo Bovi, Antonio e Andrea Talillo. *Semoventi da 47/32, 90/53 e 75/18 in Sicilia.* Ediz. illustrata - Ardite edizioni 2021.
- Italia Luca S. Cristini *Carro leggero italiano L6-40 e Semovente L40 - serie TEW Soldiershop.* Italia 2023.
- Luca S. Cristini *I carri leggeri CV3 L-33-35-38 - serie TEW Soldiershop.* Italia 2022.
- Luca S. Cristini *Semovente italiani 2° vol. - serie TEW Soldiershop.* Italia 2024.

- Luca S. Cristini *Semovente 75/18 e 75/34 - serie TEW Soldiershop*. Italia 2021.
- Luca S. Cristini *Italian Medium tank M13/40, M14/41 & M15/42 - serie TEW Soldiershop*. Italia 2022.
- Paolo Crippa e Carlo Cucut. *I reparti corazzati italiani nei Balcani*, Soldiershop 2019.
- Paolo Crippa. *I reparti corazzati del R.E. E l'armistizio 1° Volume*, Soldiershop 2021.
- Paolo Crippa. *I reparti corazzati del R.E. E l'armistizio 2° Volume*, Paolo Crippa. Soldiershop 2021.
- Paolo Crippa. *Il gruppo corazzato del Leoncello*, Soldiershop 2021.
- Paolo Crippa *I reparti corazzati della Repubblica Sociale Italiana 1943/1945*, Marvia Edizioni, 2006.
- Ralph A. Riccio *Carri armati italiani e veicoli da combattimento della Seconda Guerra Mondiale – Mattioli*Nico Sgarlato, *Corazzati Italiani 1939-1945*, War Set n°10, 2006.
- Ralph A. Riccio e E.Finazzer, (2015). *Italian Artillery of WW2. MMP Books, UK*
- Ugo Barlozzetti & Alberto Pirella *Mezzi dell'Esercito Italiano 1935-45*, Editoriale Olimpia, 1986.
- Lucio Ceva e Andrea Curami *"La meccanizzazione dell'Esercito fino al 1943"* Tomo I e II Roma 1994
- D. Vannucci - *Corazzati e blindati italiani dalle origini allo scoppio della seconda guerra mondiale*.
- A. Maraziti- *"L'Ariete a Bir-El Gobi"*. Storia Militare (in Italian). (Gennaio 2005). Albertelli edizioni.
- S.Di Giusto *Il gruppo corazzato "San Giusto" dal Regio Esercito alla RSI 1934-1945*, Laran Éditions, 2008.
- A.V. *Semoventi italiani in action* Delta Editrice - WestWard Edizioni
- Davide beretta - *Batterie semoventi alzo zero. Quelli di El Alamein*, Mursia
- Gabriele De Rosa, - *Storia dell'Ansaldo 6. Dall'IRI alla guerra 1930-1945*, Gius. Laterza & Figli, 1999.
- Giulio Benussi *Semicingolati, Motoveicoli e Veicoli Speciali del Regio Esercito Italiano 1919-1943* –Edizioni Intergest – 1976.

▲ The self-propelled 75/46 in beautiful camouflage colouring in front of the Ansaldo works.

ALREADY PUBLISHED TITLES
ALL BOOKS IN THE SERIES ARE PRINTED IN ENGLISH OR ITALIAN

VISIT OUR WEBSITE FOR MORE INFORMATION ON THE WEAPONS ENCYCLOPAEDIA:
https://soldiershop.com/collane/libri/the-weapons-encyclopaedia/

www.ingramcontent.com/pod-product-compliance
Lightning Source LLC
LaVergne TN
LVHW072118060526
838201LV00068B/4914